SCIENCE NOW! 2

Ann Fullick

Ian Richardson

David Sang

Martin Stirrup

Contents

How to use this book   1

Unit 1 Keeping fit

a	Getting around	2
b	Not bones alone	4
c	Getting fit	6
d	Huffing and puffing	8
e	Inside the lungs	10
f	No wonder smokers cough	12
g	Body transport	14
h	Moving stuff about	16
	Extras	18

Unit 2 Elements and compounds

a	Atoms and molecules	22
b	The elements	24
c	Mixtures and compounds	26
d	More about compounds	28
e	It's a mixed up world	30
f	More about elements	32
	Extras	34

Unit 3 Magnets

a	Attracting and repelling	36
b	Magnetic fields	38
c	The Earth's field	40
d	Electromagnets	42
e	Using electromagnets	44
	Extras	46

Unit 4 Adaptation

a	Home sweet home	48
b	Round pegs in round holes	50
c	All change	52
d	Chains, pyramids and biomass	54
e	Helping and hindering	56
f	How many fleas on a hedgehog?	58
g	A question of balance	60
h	Babies mean success	62
	Extras	64

Unit 5 Solar system

a	Once a day	66
b	Around the Sun	68
c	All in a year	70
d	Hot stars, cold planets	72
e	Exploring space	74
	Extras	76

Unit 6 Acids and alkalis

a	Suck a lemon!	78
b	Telling them apart	80
c	Cancelling out	82
d	Making salts	84
e	Bubbling and fizzing	86
f	Acids on the rocks	88
g	Acids and metals	90
	Extras	92

Unit 7 Using food

a	All cut up	94
b	The digestion machine	96
c	The breakdown gang	98
d	Keep the best	100
e	Using what you've got	102
	Extras	104

Unit 8 Speed

a	Travelling fast	106
b	Measuring speed	108
c	Faster and slower	110
	Extras	112

Unit 9 Chemicals in action

a	Chemicals you need	114
b	Ringing the changes	116
c	Fossil sunshine	118
d	Acid rain	120
e	Protecting metals	122
f	Getting out the metals	124
g	Pushing out the metals	126
	Extras	128

Unit 10 Energy resources

a	Ancient energy	130
b	Island in the Sun	132
c	Wet and windy	134
d	The great escape	136
e	Hotter and colder	138
	Extras	140

Glossary 142

Heinemann Educational Publishers,
Halley Court, Jordan Hill, Oxford OX2 8EJ
a division of Reed Educational & Professional Publishing Ltd

MELBOURNE AUCKLAND FLORENCE
PRAGUE MADRID ATHENS SINGAPORE
TOKYO SAO PAULO CHICAGO PORTSMOUTH (NH)
MEXICO IBADAN GABORONE JOHANNESBURG
KAMPALA NAIROBI

© Ann Fullick, Ian Richardson, David Sang, Martin Stirrup, 1996

Copyright notice
All rights reserved. No part of this publication may be reproduced, stored in a retrieval system, or transmitted in any form or by any means, electronic, mechanical, photocopying, recording, or otherwise without either the prior written permission of the Publishers or a licence permitting restricted copying in the United Kingdom issued by the Copyright Licensing Agency Ltd, 90 Tottenham Court Road, London W1P 9HE.

First published 1996

ISBN 0 435 50686 2 (hardback)
2000 99 98 97 96
10 9 8 7 6 5 4 3 2

ISBN 0435 50685 4 (softback)
2000 99 98 97 96
10 9 8 7 6 5 4 3 2

Designed and typeset by Plum Creative

Origination By Reacta Graphics

Illustrated by John Plumb, Lynda Knott, Jack Haynes, Tony Wilkins, Andrew Tewson, Dave Marshall, Olivia Brown, Shirley Tourret, John Lobhan, Jeremy Gower, Donald Harley, Martin Griffin, Dave Glover and Nicholas Beresford-Davies

Cover design by Miller, Craig and Cocking

Cover photo by Telegraph Colour Library

Printed and bound in Great Britain by Bath Colour Books, Glasgow

Acknowledgements
The authors and publishers would like to thank the following for permission to use photographs:

p 2: Science Source/SPL. p 4: Colorsport. p 5: Roger Scruton. p 6 T: Meg Sullivan. p 6 B: ACE/Ian Spratt. p 8: Roger Scruton. p 11 T: Action-Plus/R Francis. p 11 B: Tony Stone Images/Mike McQueen. p 12: Health Education Authority. p 13: The Advertising Archives. p 15: SPL/Eric Grave. p 16: ACE/Edmund Nagele. p 18 T: ZEFA. p 18 B: SPL. p 20: SPL/Matt Meadows, Peter Arnold. p 22: Oxford Scientific Films. p 24 TL, TR, BR: Roger Scruton. p24 BL: SPL/Sinclair Stammus. p 25 R: SPL/Andy Clare. p25 L: SPL/John Sonford. p 26: Roger Scruton. p 28 BM: ZEFA. p 28 rest: Roger Scruton. p 29, p 30: Roger Scruton. p 31 TL: Oxford Scientific Films/Andy Pack. p 31 TR, BL, BR: Roger Scruton. p 32 T: J Allan Cash. p 32 B: Rex Features. p 33 TL, TM, TR, BM: Roger Scruton. p 33 BL, BR: Peter Gould. p 35: J Allan Cash. p 36 T: Meg Sullivan. p 36 B, p 38, p 39: Roger Scruton. p 40 T: Colorsport. p 40 B: Roger Scruton. p 42: SPL. p 43: Peter Gould. p 44: Sue Ford/Western Eye Hospital. p 45: Peter Gould. p 48 T: SPL/PLI/ESA. p 48 ML: NHPA/Anthony Bannister. p 48 MR: NHPA/Norbert Wu. p 48 BL: NHPA/Martin Wendler. p 48 BR: Ardea. p 51 TL: NHPA/Manfred Danegger. p 51 TR: NHPA/Christophe Ratier. p 51 BL: NHPA/Michael Leach. p 51 BR: NHPA/Stephen Kraseman. p 52: NHPA/David Woodfall. p 53: Oxford Scientific Films/Philip Tull. p 56 T: FLPA/Roger Tidman. p56 B: Oxford Scientific Films/Martyn Chillmaid. p 57: Tony Stone Images/Margaret Gowan. p 58 T: Ardea. p 58 B: NHPA/Stephen Dalton. p 61 T: NHPA/David Woodfall. p 61 B: NHPA/Phillipa Scott. p 62, p 63 T: NHPA/Eric Soder. p 63 B: NHPA/William Paton. p 67: SPL/Jerry Schad. p 72 T: SPL/NASA. p 72 B: SPL/David Nunut. p 73 L: SPL/Jerry Schad. p 73 R: SPL/John Sandford. p 74 T: SPL/ESA. p 74 B: SPL/National Remote Sensing Centre. p 78: Meg Sullivan. p 83: Oxford Scientific Films/Ben Osborne. p 84 TL, TR: Roger Scruton. p 84 B1: Courtesy of Standard Fireworks. p84 B2: Roger Scruton. p 84 B3: SPL/Larry Mulvehill. p 84 B4, M: Roger Scruton. p 84 B5: Peter Gould. p 86: Peter Gould. p 87: Peter Gould. p 88 T: Ardea. p88 B: SPL/Robert Knowles. p 89 T: Oxford Scientific Films/Geoff Kidd. p 89 B: Heather Angel. p 91: Hulton Deutsch. p 92: SPL/Dr Jeremy Burgess. p 93 T, M: Roger Scruton. p 93 B: J Allan Cash. p 95 R: FLPA/Fritz Polking. p 95 T: Only Horses. p 95 L: Bruce Coleman Ltd/Rod Williams. p 96: SPL/Francoise Sauze. p 98: Roger Scruton. p 100: SPL/David Scharf. p 101 T: Roger Scruton. p 101 B: Unicef. p 103A: Natural Science Photos/S. Bharaj. p 103B: Natural Science Photos/C. Mattison. p 103C: Natural Science Photos/Hal Beraj. p 103D: Natural Science Photos/W. Care. p 103E: NHPA/Tsuneo Nakamura. p 106 T: ACE Photo. p 106 B: Allsport. p 107 T: Meg Sullivan. p 107 B: Action Plus/Peter Tarny. p 108: Meg Sullivan. p 109: Data Harvest Educational Electronics. p 110 T: Allsport Anton Want. p 110 B: Roger Scruton. p 116 T: Tony Stone Image. p 116 B: Meg Sullivan. p 117: J Allan Cash. p 118 T: Tony Stone Image. p 118 M: GSF. p 118 B: Courtesy British Gas. p 119 L: Roger Scruton. p 119 T: Solid Fuel Association. p 119 B: Courtesy British Gas. p 119 R: Camping Gaz (GB). p 120 T: Environmental Pic Lib. p 120 M: Peter Gould. p 120 B: SPL/Jerry Mason. p 121: Roger Scruton. p 122 T: Sally & Richard Greenhill. p122 M, B: Roger Scruton. p 123 T: Tony Stone Image. p 123 B: Roger Scruton. p 124 T: SPL/Arnold Fisher. p 124 M, BL, BR: Peter Gould. p 125 T: ZEFA. p125 B, p 126 TL, TR: Roger Scruton. p 126 ML: SPL/Arnold Fisher. p 126 MR, BL: Roger Scruton. p 126 BR: ZEFA. p128: Hulton Deutsch. p129: Barry Lewis/Network. p 130 T: NHPA. p 130 M: ACE. p130 B: J Allan Cash. p 132: SPL/Peter Menzel. p 134 T: J Allan Cash. p 134 B: Waterway Images. p 137 TL: SPL/Martin Bond. p 137 TR: Environmental Picture Library/Martin Bond. p 137 ML, MR: Microscopix. p 137 B: Bryan & Cherry Alexander. p 139: SPL/James Stevenson.

The publishers have made every effort to trace the copyright holders, but if they have inadvertently overlooked any, they will be pleased to make the necessary arrangements at the first opportunity.

How to use this book

Welcome to **Science Now!** We have tried to make the book as easy to use and understand as possible. Here are a few notes to help you find your way around.

The book has ten units. Each unit covers one of the big ideas of science in biology, physics or chemistry. Biology units are green, physics units are red, chemistry units are blue.

What's in a unit?

The units are organised into double-page spreads. Each spread has:

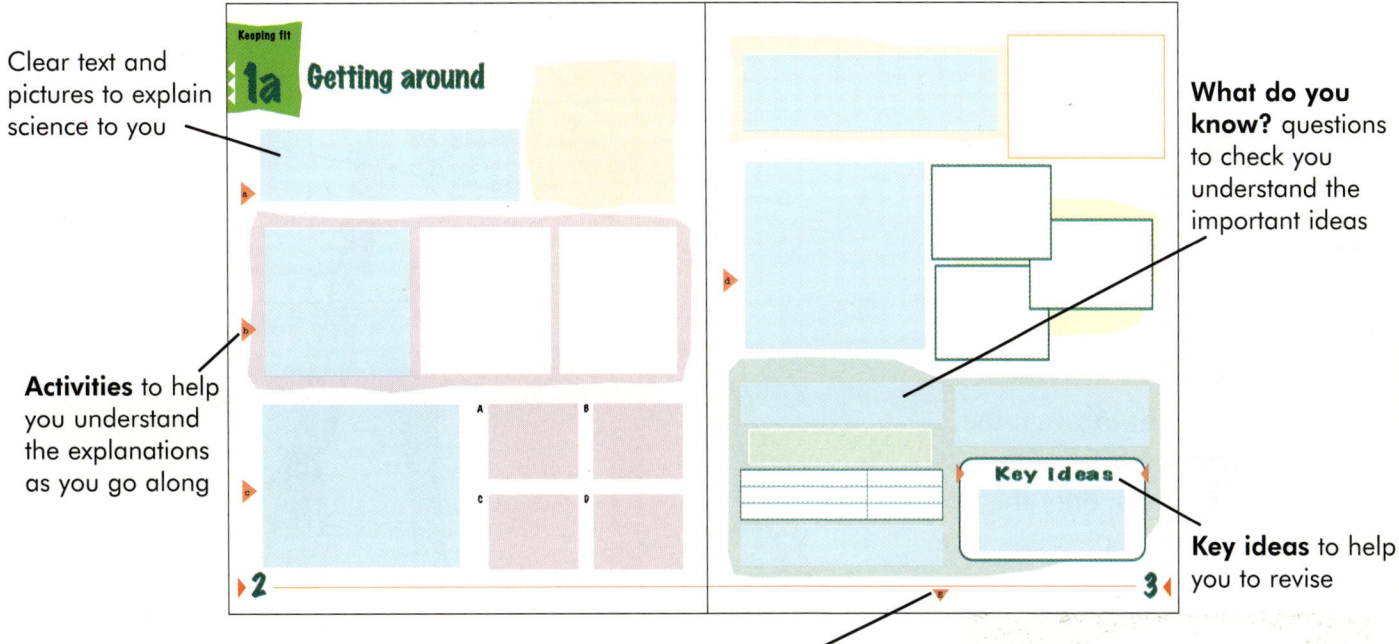

Clear text and pictures to explain science to you

Activities to help you understand the explanations as you go along

What do you know? questions to check you understand the important ideas

Key ideas to help you to revise

If you finish quickly, some spreads also have a section of interesting new ideas and things to do in the **Extras** pages at the end of the unit

None of the activities needs special equipment or preparation. All the practical activities for the course are in the photocopiable Activities and Assessment Pack which goes with the book.

Glossary

At the back of the book you will find a list of important scientific words and their meanings, so that you can remind yourself quickly of what they mean. If you want any more information you can look at the pages whose numbers are next to the words.

We hope you find **Science Now!** useful in your course. Above all, we hope that you enjoy it!

Keeping fit

1a Getting around

All living organisms move, including people. We are vertebrates with a bony skeleton inside our bodies. We use that skeleton to help us move about.

The inside story

If we can see our bones, we can understand better what they do. To see the bones inside our bodies we use X-ray photographs.

X-rays go straight through the soft parts of our bodies. On X-ray photographs, only the hard bones show up.

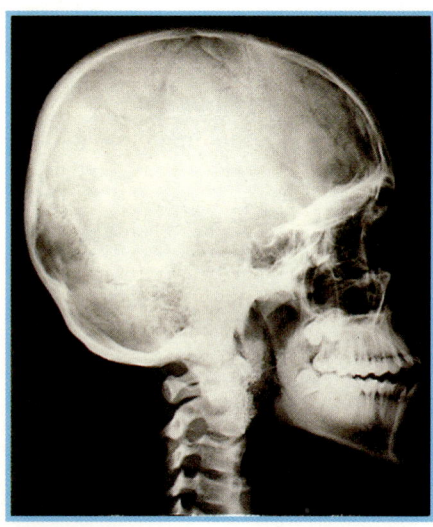

X-ray photographs let us see the bones inside a living body.

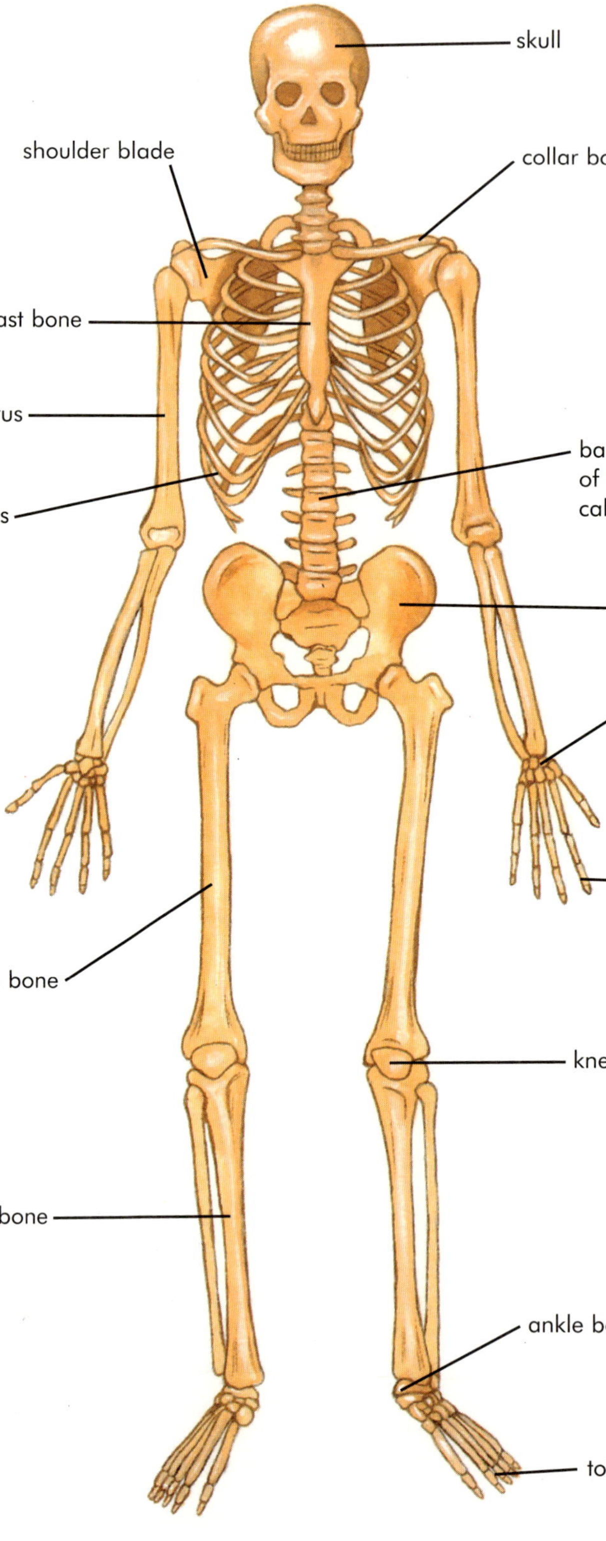

- skull
- shoulder blade
- collar bone
- breast bone
- humerus
- ribs
- backbone made up of lots of small bones called vertebrae
- pelvis
- wrist bones
- finger bones
- thigh bone
- kneecap
- shin bone
- ankle bones
- toe bones

2

Supporting and protecting us

Without a strong **support** system to hold us up we would all be giant, rubbery blobs! Our bones are made of a strong but slightly flexible material, which holds us up well.

The delicate parts of our bodies, like our brains and our hearts, need **protection**. The skull and the ribs are strong bony cages which protect our brains and our hearts.

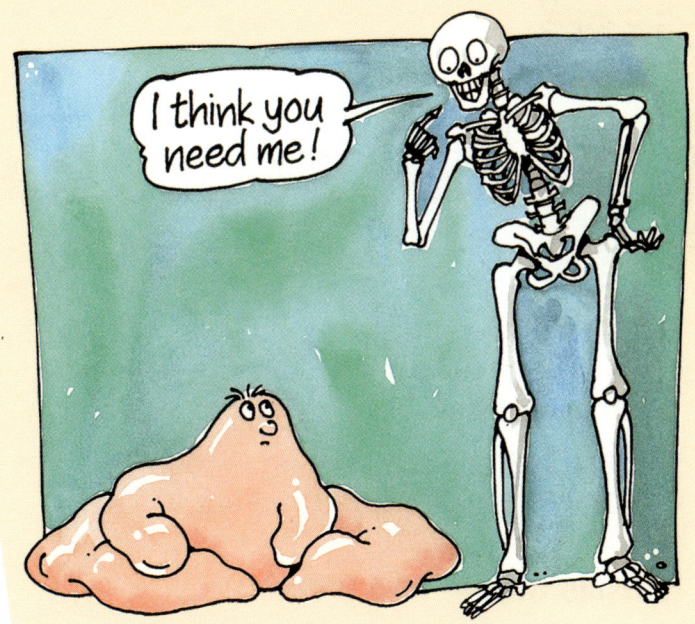

Moving us

We need to be able to move about quickly and easily. A place where two bones meet is called a **joint**. The bones of the skeleton move at the joints, and this is how we move our bodies.

What do you know?

1 Here are some of the bones of the body. Use them to answer the following questions.

| ribs   skull   backbone (vertebrae) |
| shin bone   thigh bone   toe bones |

a Which bits of the skeleton hold the body upright?
b Which bits of the skeleton protect delicate organs?

2 The skeleton is not one single large bone. It is made up of lots of small bones with joints between them. Why?

3 The bones of babies and small children are more flexible than those of an adult. This allows them to keep growing.
a Apart from allowing growth, why is it a good thing that small children's bones are quite flexible?
b Adults would not get on very well if their bones were as bendy as those of a small child. Why not?

Key ideas

The human skeleton is made up of lots of bones. We can see bones using X-ray photographs.

The skeleton does three main jobs.

It **supports** the body.

It **protects** delicate organs.

It is **jointed** so we can move easily.

Keeping fit

1b Not bones alone

The bones of your skeleton can move, but only if you make them.

a Pick up your pen and lift it up to your shoulder. Which bones did you move?

Athletes train to get big, strong muscles which are easy to see.

Muscle men – and women

To move our bones we need muscles. Muscles are made up of fibres, which are bundles of very long cells. They are made of protein which can **contract** (shorten). A group of similar cells all working together like this is called a **tissue**.

Muscles are joined to bones by **tendons**. Each end of a muscle is joined to a different bone. When a muscle contracts, it pulls a bone into a different position.

Your muscles can only pull. Once they have pulled a bone, they can't push it back again. Another muscle must contract to pull it back. While the second muscle contracts, the first muscle **relaxes**. Muscles that work against each other in pairs like this are called **antagonistic muscles**.

b Try the arm movements shown below. See if you can feel your muscles as they shorten and stretch.

c Which other parts of your body are moved by pairs of muscles working like this?

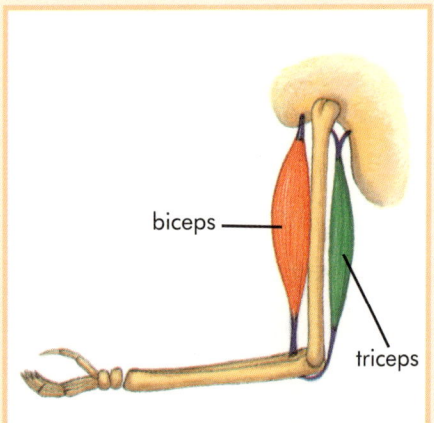

biceps
triceps

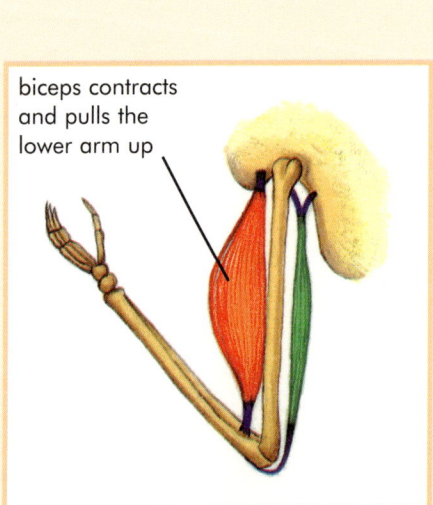

biceps contracts and pulls the lower arm up

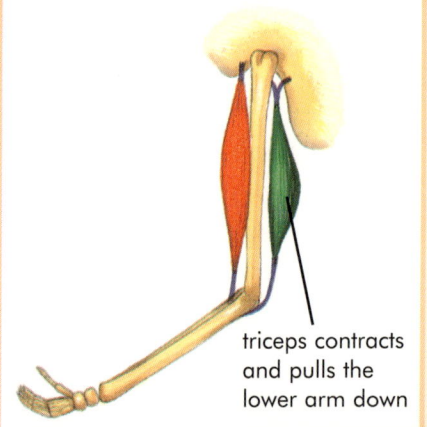

triceps contracts and pulls the lower arm down

Moving smoothly

The tread of human feet can wear away stone over hundreds of years. But in our joints, our bones move past each other all the time without wearing away.

The ends of our bones are covered with tough, rubbery **cartilage** to protect them. In joints where the bones move a lot, like hips, knees and elbows, **synovial fluid** cushions and **lubricates** the joint. This fluid makes sure that the bones move smoothly without grinding against each other, doing the same job as oil in the engine of a car.

The bones are held together in a joint by strong straps called **ligaments**.

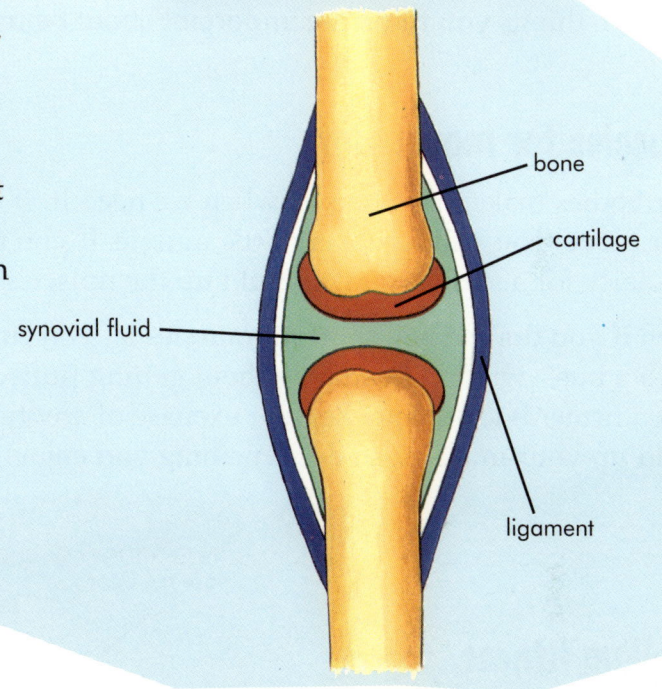

What do you know?

1 Copy and complete the following sentences. Use the words below to fill the gaps.

| antagonistic | muscles | tendons |
| skeleton | pull | protein | contract |

The bones of the _____ are moved by _____ made of _____. The muscles are attached to the bones by _____. When muscles _____, they shorten and _____ on the bones to move them. Muscles come in _____ pairs.

2 Copy the diagram of a joint. Label each part of the joint and describe what it does.

3 The muscle that lifts your arm up (your biceps) is bigger than the muscle that pulls your arm down (your triceps). Can you think of a scientific explanation for this?

Key ideas

The bones are moved by muscles **contracting**.

Muscles can only pull, so they work in **antagonistic pairs**.

The bones are cushioned and protected at joints by **cartilage**. In joints which move a lot, they are also lubricated by **synovial fluid**.

Keeping fit

1c Getting fit

We are often encouraged to 'get fit and stay fit'. But what do we mean by getting fit?

a List five things you think are important about being fit.

Muscles for movement

Our bodies make more muscle when we need it. If you hardly ever move, you will have very little muscle. If you train regularly for a sport, you will build up the muscles you need.

Even if you don't enjoy sport, fit muscles let you run fast to catch a bus, swim on holiday without getting puffed, and give you a firmer body shape. Regular exercise of any type helps to build up your muscles, so do something you enjoy!

Fuelling fitness

When you exercise, your muscles are working hard. They need energy, which comes from respiration. Working muscles need plenty of glucose (sugar) and oxygen for respiration. So exercise is not only about the muscles and moving your skeleton. Most of your body gets involved when you exercise.

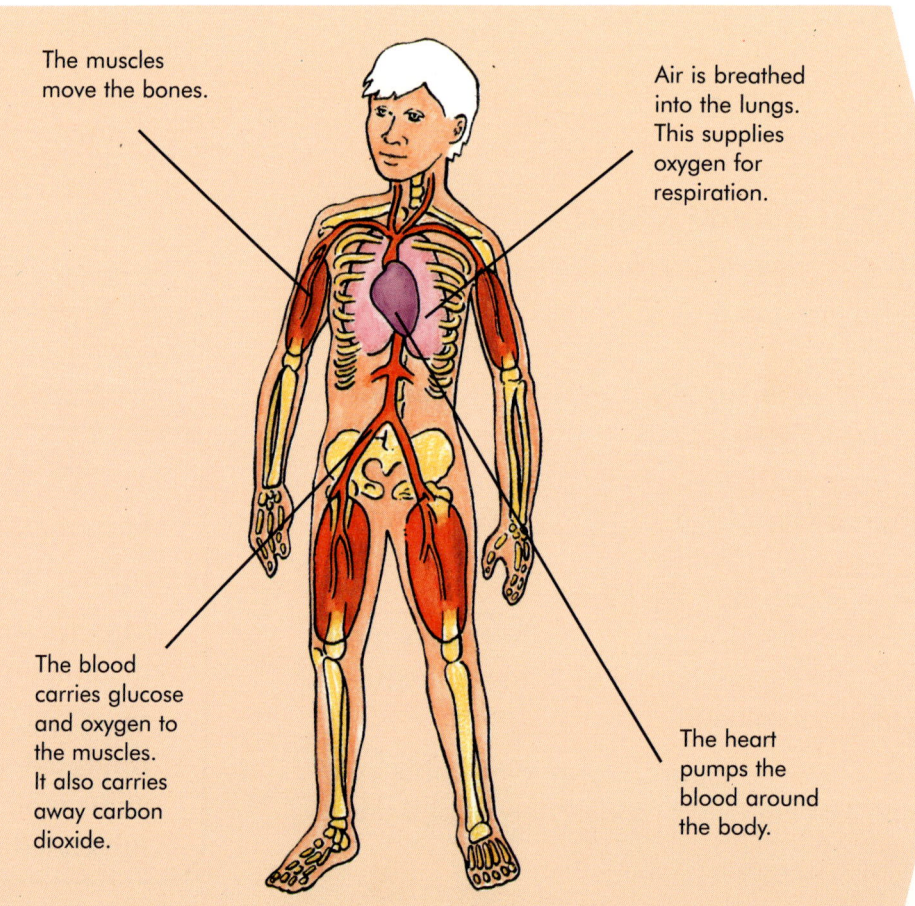

The muscles move the bones.

Air is breathed into the lungs. This supplies oxygen for respiration.

The blood carries glucose and oxygen to the muscles. It also carries away carbon dioxide.

The heart pumps the blood around the body.

6

Extra oxygen

You get oxygen from the air you breathe. When you exercise you need more oxygen, so you breathe more. If you are not very fit, you soon get puffed because you can't get enough air. But as you practise and get fitter, your lungs get bigger. You breathe more deeply, which gives you a much better oxygen supply. You can exercise more without getting so puffed.

Have a heart!

Your blood carries glucose and oxygen to your muscles. As your muscles work and respire, they produce carbon dioxide waste. The blood carries this away from the muscles. Your heart pumps blood around your body all the time.

When you first start exercising, your heart pounds with the effort. But your heart is made of muscle. When it has to work hard regularly, it gets bigger and stronger. It beats more strongly and efficiently as you get fit. It can supply all the food and oxygen you need without thumping too hard and too fast.

Fitness affects your whole body. If you are fit it is easier to cope with the demands of being alive.

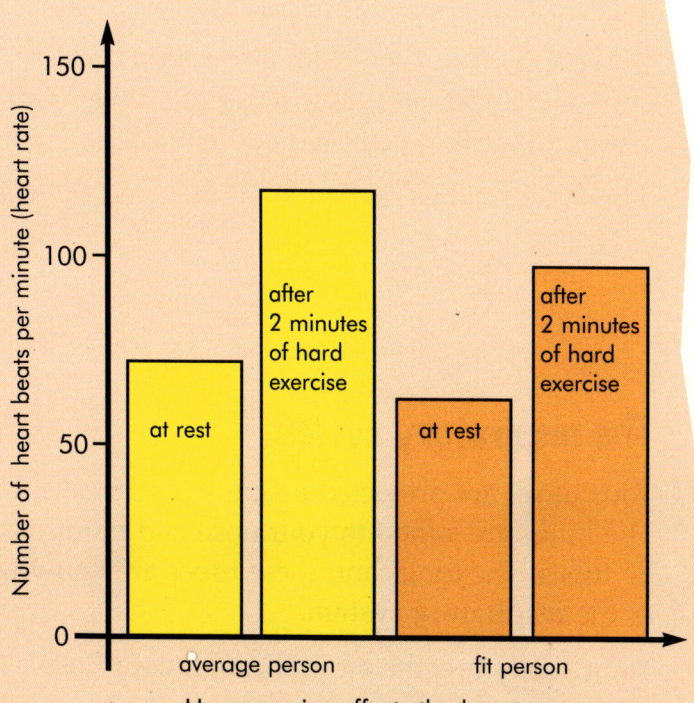

How exercise affects the heart rate

b Look at the bar chart. Whose heart beats faster after exercise, the average person's or the fit person's?

What do you know?

1 When you run to catch up with your friends, what happens to:
a your muscles   **b** your breathing   **c** your heart?

2 Which parts of your body would build up extra muscle if you took up:
a football   **b** swimming   **c** weightlifting?

3 A fit person and an unfit person are sitting reading quietly together. The fit person's heart beats more slowly than the unfit person's heart. Also, the fit person breathes fewer times each minute. Why is this?

Key ideas

Muscles use glucose and oxygen for energy when they contract.

The blood carries glucose and oxygen to the muscles.

The heart pumps blood round the body. During exercise, it pumps faster.

You need more oxygen during exercise, so you breathe faster.

A fit person copes better with the demands of exercise.

Keeping fit

1d Huffing and puffing

All living things **respire**. They use oxygen to get energy from their food.

You get your oxygen from the air you breathe. You breathe air into your lungs and take in oxygen. When you breathe out, you are getting rid of carbon dioxide waste.

a How many times do you breathe in and out each minute?

The respiratory system

Your lungs are protected inside your rib cage. The lungs are joined to your nose and mouth by tubes. The lungs and these tubes are known as the **respiratory system**.

You usually breathe air in through your nose. The inside of your nose is warm, wet and hairy. The air coming in gets warm and moist. It is cleaned as dust is trapped in the hairs.

The air goes down the **windpipe**. This tube is lined with tiny hairs called **cilia** which move dust and dirt up away from the lungs. In the chest, the windpipe divides into two **bronchi**. These split into smaller and smaller tubes. The air travels along these tubes into the lungs. When you breathe out, the air travels back the way it came, but it often leaves your body through your mouth instead of your nose.

b We use the air we breathe to make sounds as well as to give us oxygen. How do we do it? Try 'talking' using the air you breathe in and the air you breathe out. Which works best?

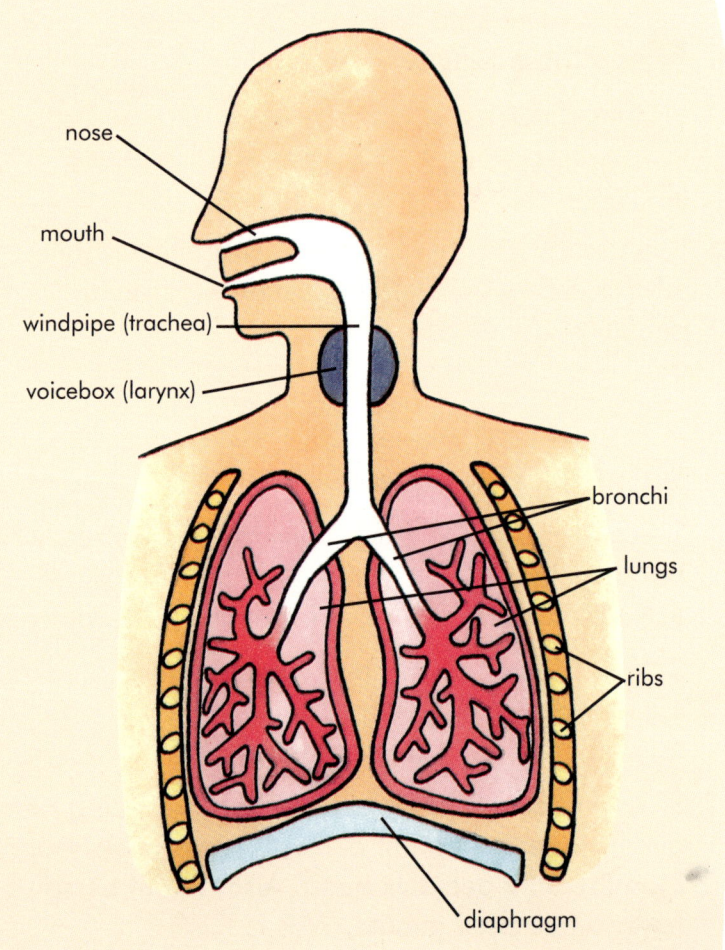

Breathe in, breathe out

c Put your hands on your ribs. Breathe in deeply, then breathe out hard, and write down what happens to your ribs.

When you breathe in, special muscles lift your ribs upwards and outwards. The diaphragm muscle contracts and flattens. The space inside your chest gets bigger, and so air moves into your lungs. You breathe in.

When you breathe out, the diaphragm muscle and the muscles between the ribs all relax. The ribs move down and the diaphragm domes upwards. This makes the space in the chest smaller again, and air is squeezed out of the lungs. You breathe out.

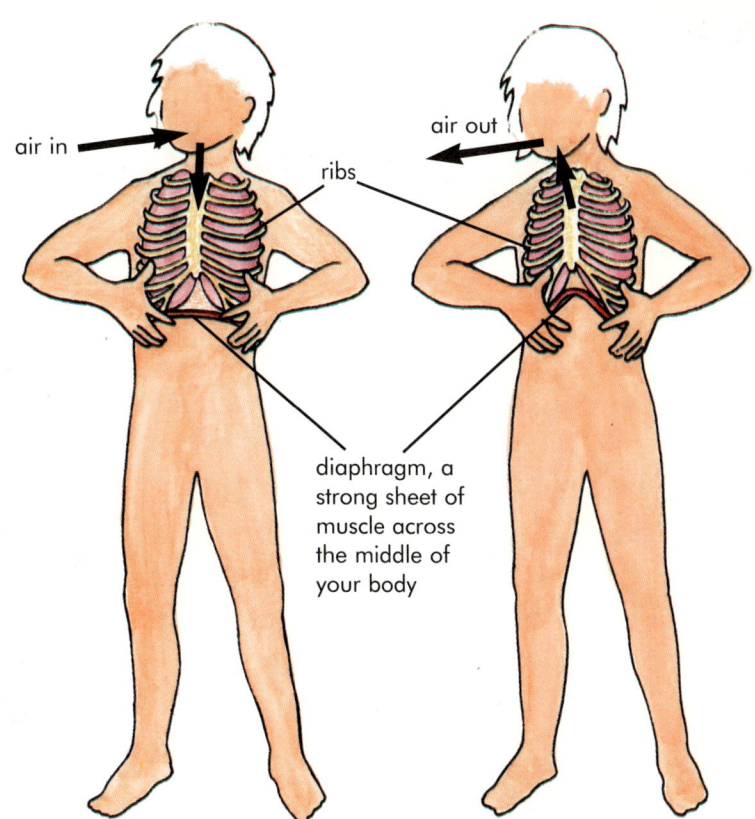

What do you know?

1 Write these sentences in the correct order to explain how you breathe in and out.
a The muscles of the ribs and diaphragm relax so the space in your chest gets smaller and the air is squeezed out. You breathe out.
b The warm, moist air from the windpipe goes into the bronchi and on into the tiny tubes of the lungs.
c Oxygen is taken from the air into the blood in the lungs. Waste carbon dioxide is removed from the blood to the air.
d When you breathe in, the muscles of the ribs and diaphragm contract to make the space inside your chest bigger.
e Air moves in through your nose, and then passes down the windpipe.

2 If your nose is blocked, you may breathe in through your mouth. This is not as good for you as breathing in through your nose. What are the problems for:
a the lungs **b** the whole body?

3 What happens to your ribs and your diaphragm when you breathe in? Copy and complete the table.

Activity	Ribs	Diaphragm
a breathing in		
b breathing out		

Key ideas

We breathe in and out, taking in oxygen from the air and getting rid of carbon dioxide.

The **respiratory system** is made up of the lungs and the tubes linking the lungs to the mouth and nose.

Air is moved in and out of the lungs by movements of the ribs and diaphragm.

Keeping fit

1e Inside the lungs

People often imagine their lungs like two pink balloons which fill with air and then empty as they breathe. But in fact your lungs are much more like a pair of pink sponges.

a You need to get as much oxygen out of the air as possible. Why do you think sponges might be better for this than balloons?

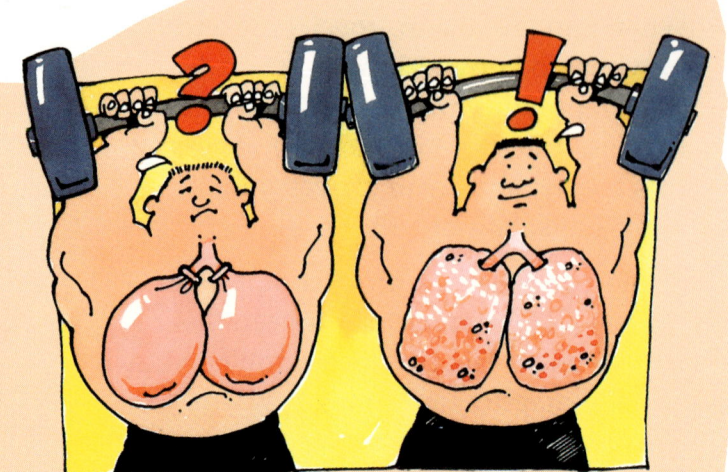

Air sacs in the lungs

Each of your lungs is made up of millions of tiny air sacs called **alveoli**. These are what make the lungs look like sponges. There are tiny blood vessels surrounding the alveoli. The alveoli have very thin walls so that the air and the blood are as close to each other as possible. Oxygen goes from the air into the blood. Carbon dioxide goes from the blood into the air to be breathed out. This **gas exchange** takes place every time you breathe.

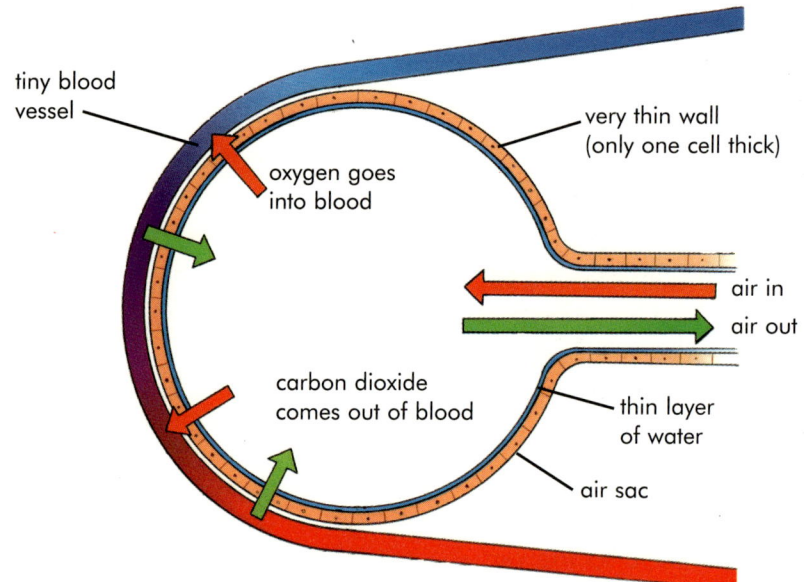

One of the air sacs or alveoli in the lungs

What a lot of lung!

We need lots of oxygen for respiration to supply all the energy we need. We also have to get rid of the carbon dioxide produced in respiration, otherwise the carbon dioxide would poison us. The little alveoli give our lungs an enormous surface area. Oxygen and carbon dioxide are exchanged over this large surface. In one lung we have about 300 million alveoli. If all the alveoli in both the lungs could be spread out flat, they would cover a tennis court!

10

More oxygen please!

b 1 Count how many times you breathe in one minute and make a note of it.

2 Predict what would happen to the number of breaths you take in a minute if you walked round the lab for two minutes.

3 What do you think would happen if you jogged hard on the spot for a minute?

The amount of oxygen we need varies with what we do. If we need more oxygen for exercise, we breathe more deeply. Air gets into more of the alveoli. We also breathe more quickly, so the alveoli fill and empty more often.

Sometimes people need so much extra oxygen that their lungs get bigger.

If you exercise hard regularly, your lungs get bigger so you can get enough oxygen.

High up in the mountains, the air has less oxygen. People who live high up have very big lungs.

What do you know?

1 Copy and complete the following sentences. Use the words below to fill the gaps.

> air   alveoli   vessels   oxygen
> blood   surface area

The lungs are made up of tiny air sacs called _____. The air sacs have thin moist walls and a large _____ _____. They are close to tiny blood _____ which makes gas exchange easy. _____ leaves the air and goes into the blood, while carbon dioxide leaves the _____ and goes into the _____ to be breathed out.

2a Why do people who live high up have bigger lungs than people who live at sea level?
b Pearl divers stay below water for several minutes at a time searching for oysters on the sea bed. They manage without using air tanks, because they have very big lungs. Can you give a scientific explanation for this?

3 If you suffer from asthma, the tubes leading into your lungs get narrower. When you have a bad chest cold, the tubes leading to the alveoli produce lots of thick sticky mucus. Both of these illnesses make you feel short of breath because you can't get enough oxygen. Explain why each illness makes it hard to get oxygen.

Key ideas

The lungs are made up of tiny air sacs called **alveoli**.

Gas exchange takes place in the alveoli. Oxygen goes from the air into the blood and carbon dioxide goes from the blood into the air.

The alveoli have thin walls and are moist. There are blood vessels close to them. The alveoli give the lungs a big surface area. All this allows gas exchange to take place.

Keeping fit

1f No wonder smokers cough

The lungs of a newborn baby are pink and clean. But the lungs of smokers are grey. With each cigarette, they take smoke carrying tar down into their lungs. The smoke stops the air-cleaning system of the lungs working properly.

What is tar?

Tar is a thick, sticky black substance. It goes right into the delicate alveoli. As tar builds up, the alveoli are damaged. Their thin walls get thicker until they are too thick for gas exchange to take place properly.

Tar also causes other problems in the lungs. Some of the chemicals in tar can cause cancer. Cancer happens when cells grow quickly but don't work properly. Lung cancer is a very dangerous sort of cancer. It can grow 'silently' in the lung without causing problems until it is too late to cure.

a Look at the bar chart. How does smoking affect your chances of getting lung cancer?

Any other problems?

Cancer of the mouth and throat are also more common in smokers. But cancer isn't the only health risk from smoking. The lungs become thinner and weaker. The alveoli break down to form larger sacs, which fill up with fluid. This is emphysema. It makes people 'drown' in their own lungs.

Smokers also get coughs, shortness of breath and lots of phlegm. And as well as damaging the lungs, smoking is very bad for the heart.

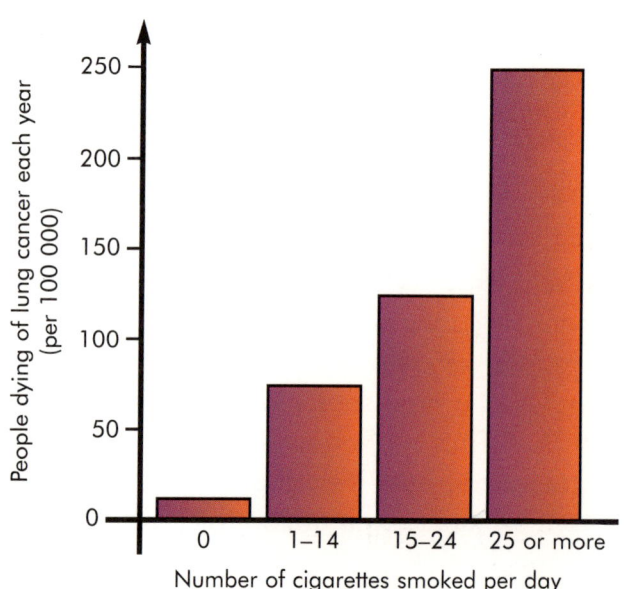

Sleeping cilia

The cilia in your respiratory system move dirt and mucus out of the tubes, keeping your lungs pink and clean. But tobacco smoke stops the cilia working. Now not only tar but also other dirt and mucus get down into the lungs. It really is no wonder smokers cough!

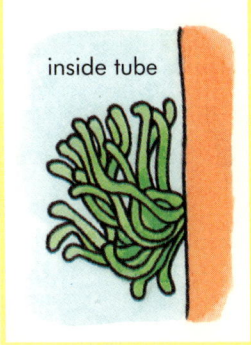
Active cilia beat to move mucus and dirt out of the lungs.

After smoking, the cilia are limp and inactive.

Only old people get ill!

Lots of young people smoke. When you're young, it's easy to ignore warnings from adults about your future health. But young or old, every cigarette has an effect. Your alveoli can't get as much oxygen if they are battling with tar, and they can't get rid of carbon dioxide so easily either. Smoking makes you smell like a stale ashtray. It also stops you being so good at sport or dancing or cycling or climbing the stairs. Lungs and smoking just don't go together.

No more smoke, no more damage

Even if you don't smoke yourself, you can still be damaged by breathing in smoke from other people's cigarettes. This is called passive smoking. But as soon as you stop smoking, or keep away from smoky places, the damage stops. Your lungs gradually repair themselves.

People who smoke carry less oxygen in their blood. If a pregnant woman smokes, her growing baby is short of oxygen.

What do you know?

1 Name three diseases which can be caused by smoking.
2 Why does smoking make gas exchange in the lungs more difficult?
3 What effect does smoking have on the cilia in the respiratory system?
4 Write a paragraph to explain why smoking is not a good idea.

Key ideas

Cigarette smoke contains tar which can cause lung cancer.

Smoking prevents gases being exchanged in the lungs quickly. It increases the risk of many diseases.

If you stop smoking, your body can repair the damage.

Keeping fit

1g Body transport

Imagine a village like this one. A complicated transport system makes sure that the village gets everything it needs.

a Make a list of things that need to be transported in and out of a village.

Just like the village, your body has many needs. The cells of your body need food and oxygen. Carbon dioxide and other wastes need to be removed from the cells. Parts of the body need repairing, diseases need fighting and messages need carrying. How can everything be carried to and from the cells?

Red river of life

The blood and blood vessels make up the transport system of the body. This table shows you some of the things carried around the body in the blood.

What is transported?	Where is it transported?
oxygen	from the lungs to all the cells, for respiration
carbon dioxide	from all the cells to the lungs, to be removed
food	from the gut to all the cells, for respiration
waste products like urea	from all the cells to the kidneys, to be removed
chemical messages	from the places where they are made to the whole body
repair system of the body	to wherever the damage takes place
defence system of the body	to wherever bacteria enter the body

What is blood?

If you cut yourself, you bleed. A red liquid comes out of the wound. But blood is not really a red liquid at all, as a closer look using a microscope shows us.

A single drop of blood contains millions of tiny blood cells in a straw-coloured liquid. Different types of blood cells do different jobs. The liquid has its own jobs to do as well. Together they make up the blood.

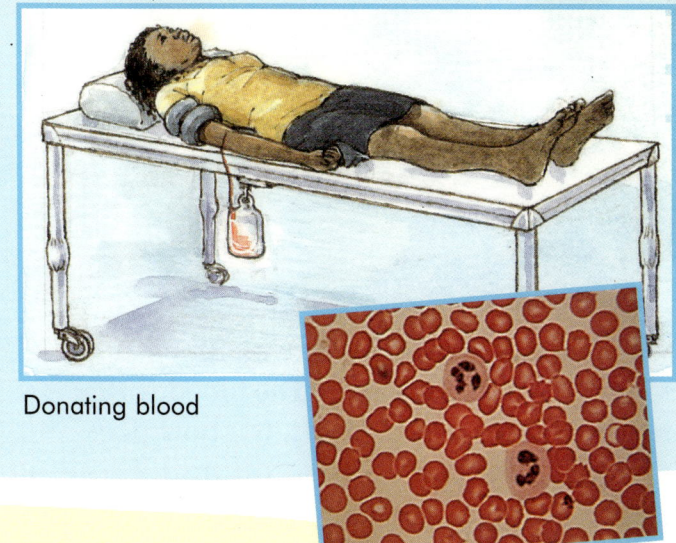

Donating blood

 **A Red blood cells** give your blood its red colour. They carry oxygen around your body.

 **B White blood cells** are bigger than red blood cells. They come in lots of shapes and sizes. Their main job is to defend your body against disease.

 **C Platelets** are tiny bits of cells. They help make clots and scabs over cuts, and repair your body.

 **D** This pale yellow liquid called **plasma** makes up most of your blood. It is mainly water. It carries dissolved food, chemical messages and waste products. Plasma also helps to make clots and scabs.

What do you know?

1 Match the words with the phrases to write five correct sentences.

Blood	carry oxygen.
White blood cells	form clots and scabs.
Red blood cells	carries dissolved substances and helps with clotting.
Platelets	defend the body against disease.
Plasma	transports cells and substances round the body.

2 Why is a transport system so important in the body?

3 Read this paragraph and answer the questions that follow:

When people are hurt in accidents or have big operations, they may be given blood. This blood has been donated by other people. Sometimes whole blood is donated, sometimes just the plasma. Great care is taken to make sure the blood doesn't clot.

a Why do you think people might need to be given blood?
b Why is it so important that the blood doesn't clot?

Key ideas

The blood transports substances around the body.

The blood is made up of **red blood cells**, **white blood cells**, **platelets** and **plasma**.

Keeping fit

1h Moving stuff about

A transport system is for moving things from one place to another. The blood is the transport system of the body, but how does it move stuff about?

a Write down how you think blood is moved around the body, then read on to see if you are right.

Have a heart!

Your heart beats about 70 times each minute throughout your life. It pumps blood to your lungs to pick up oxygen and get rid of carbon dioxide. It also pumps blood around your body, supplying the needs of all your cells and carrying away poisonous wastes.

The heart pumps your blood around a system of tubes called **blood vessels**. Some blood vessels carry oxygen-rich blood away from your heart to the body. There are called **arteries**. Other blood vessels bring blood loaded with carbon dioxide back to the heart. These are called **veins**.

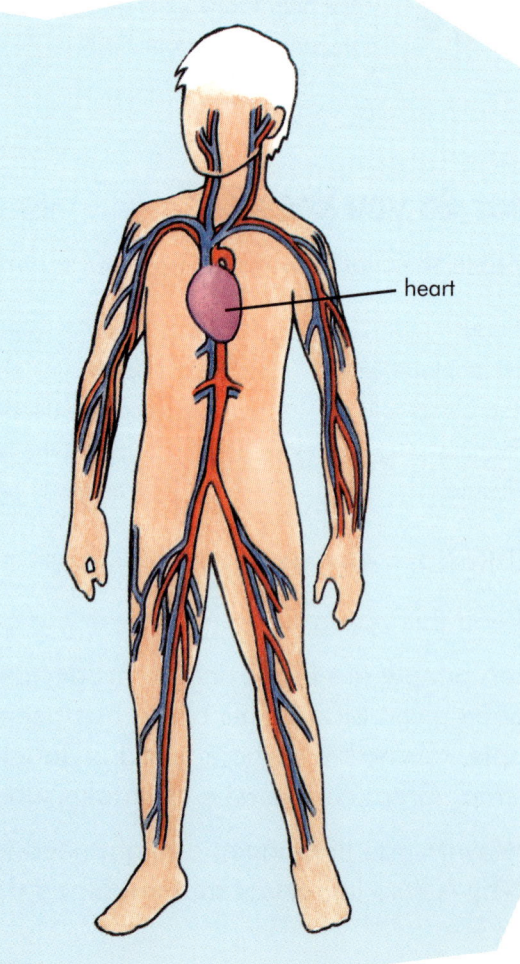

Loading and unloading

Connecting the arteries to the veins is a network of very tiny blood vessels called **capillaries**. The capillaries run through the tissues of the body, carrying substances to and from the cells. The arteries and veins are like the motorways and main roads of your body. Capillaries are like the country lanes and side streets, where substances are loaded into and out of the blood.

As the blood flows around your body, food and oxygen leave it and go to the cells. Waste products are loaded in. How does this happen?

artery | capillaries – all substances move in and out of the blood through these tiny blood vessels | vein

Blood moves quite slowly in the capillaries. Food and oxygen dissolved in the blood move into the cells that need them. At the same time, substances that are not needed in the cells move out into the blood. Substances often move from places where there is plenty of them to places where there is very little. You can see this in the drawing of the air sac.

b

1 Where is there more oxygen, in the blood or in the air sac? Which way is it moving?

2 Where is there more carbon dioxide, in the blood or in the air sac? Which way is it moving?

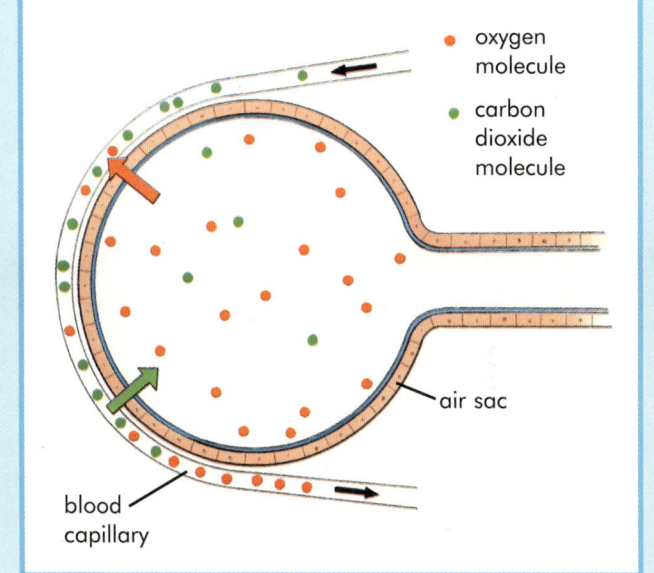

What do you know?

1 Answer these questions with full sentences.
a What pumps the blood around your body?
b Which sort of blood vessel carries oxygen-rich blood away from your heart to your body?
c Which blood vessels are very tiny and run next to the cells of your body?
d Which blood vessels carry blood loaded with carbon dioxide back to your heart?

2 Design a poster for the wall of your science lab called 'Transport in the body'.

Key ideas

The heart pumps your blood around a system of tubes called **blood vessels**.

The main types of blood vessels are the **arteries**, the **veins** and the **capillaries**.

Substances are moved between the capillaries and the cells.

Keeping fit

1 EXTRAS

1b Sticks and stones may break my bones...

Most of us have had a broken bone, or know somebody else who has. Most broken bones mend after a few weeks in a plaster cast. Human bone is constantly forming and changing, so the body can heal a clean break quickly and easily.

Sometimes damage to the skeleton is much more serious. Road accidents can shatter the bones of a limb into pieces, or badly damage joints. Doctors put the bone back together with metal plates and screws, but it takes months or even years for the bone to recover. The pins always have to stay in place.

New research has developed a special 'glue' which scientists hope to use on badly damaged bone. The glue is very strong and so much like bone that the body eventually replaces it with the real thing, giving much better healing than a metal pin.

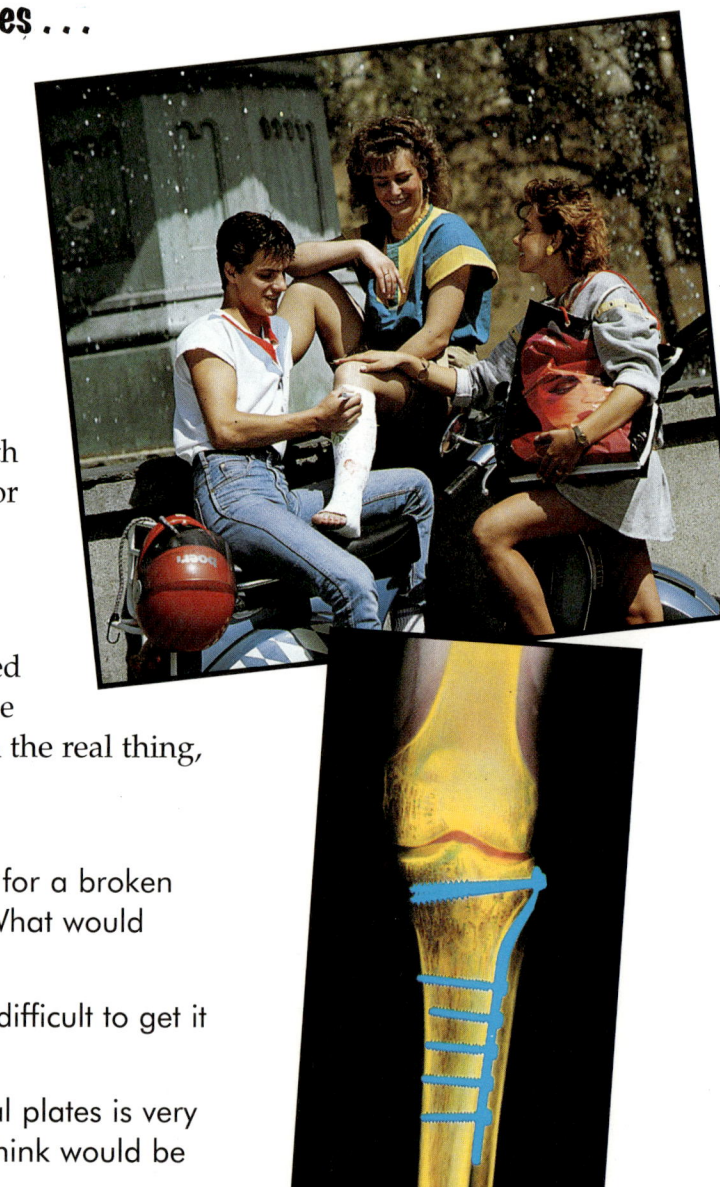

1 Why do you think that the normal treatment for a broken bone is to set it in plaster for several weeks? What would happen if the bone wasn't put in plaster?

2 If a joint is damaged, it can be particularly difficult to get it to heal. Why?

3 Piecing a shattered bone together with metal plates is very clever, but there are difficulties. What do you think would be the main problems?

4 What do you see as the big advantages of the new 'bone glue' which is being developed?

1e What causes asthma?

People with asthma suffer from wheezing and breathlessness. In asthma, the lining of the tubes leading down into the lungs swell, so that the tubes become much narrower. Asthma is the only major disease that is becoming more and more common in children. What causes it?

No one knows for sure, so there isn't a simple answer. If your parents have asthma, it is more likely that you will too. If your family are smokers, you are more likely to suffer. Asthma is often caused by an allergy, perhaps to house dust mites, or a particular food, or the fur of your pet. The increase in fumes from cars has also been blamed for the increase in asthma sufferers.

Asthma can usually be controlled well by drugs. Asthma sufferers need to carry inhalers with them all the time, in case they get an attack. Without treatment, asthma can kill.

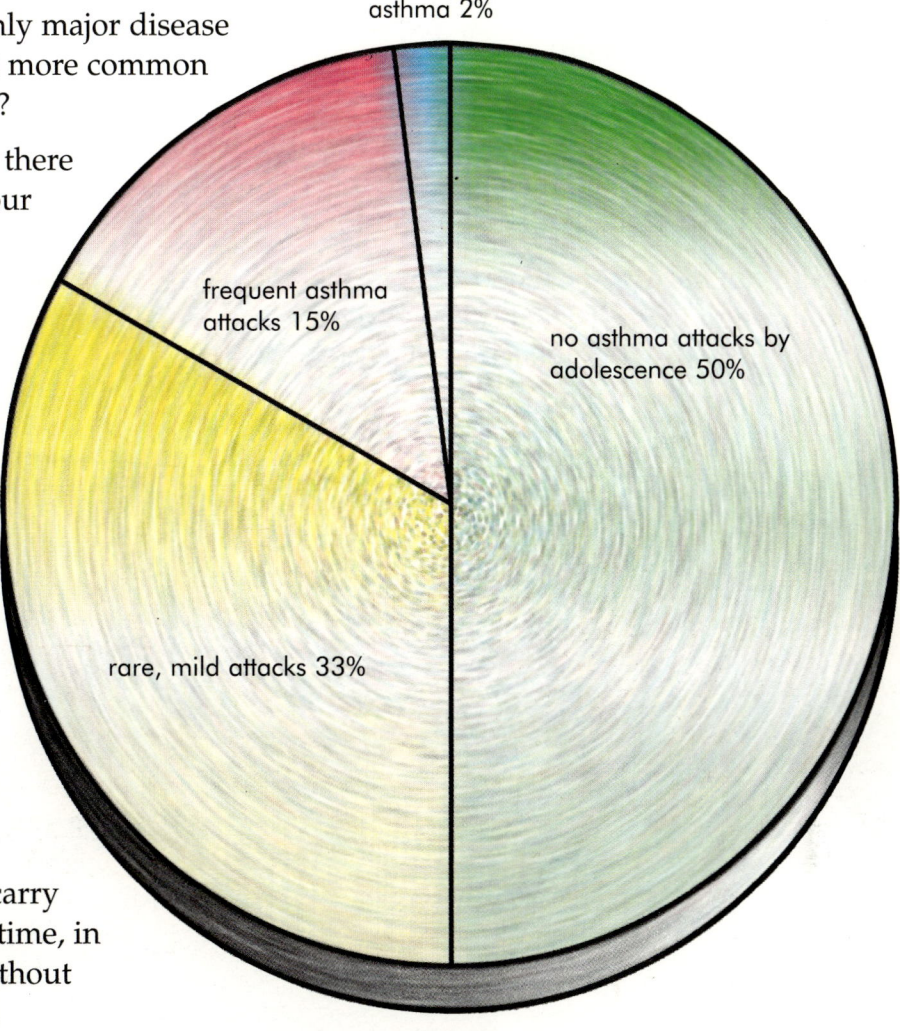

Pie chart showing how many people have asthma

1a What percentage of teenagers have never had an asthma attack?
b What percentage of people who develop asthma as children will go on to have frequent asthma attacks as adults?

2 Prepare a leaflet to give to the parents of small children who have just had their first asthma attack. Explain what asthma is and its possible causes. Try and give some simple advice about how they might help avoid future attacks.

The pulse of life

Every time your heart beats, it pumps blood into your arteries and around your body. The pressure of blood in your arteries is quite high. You can feel this when you take your pulse. After the beat, your heart must fill up with blood before it can pump again, and so the pressure of blood in your arteries is lower.

When a doctor measures your blood pressure, she measures the pressure both when the heart is pumping and when it is filling. If the measurements are higher than expected, you have **high blood pressure**.

Smoking can narrow the blood vessels, making it harder for the heart to force blood through them. The table shows the number of people per thousand who die early from diseases related to high blood pressure.

Blood pressure and smoking	Number of early deaths per thousand people
normal blood pressure/non-smoker	1
normal blood pressure/smoker	2
high blood pressure/non-smoker	2
high blood pressure/smoker	5

1 Draw a bar chart of this data.

2 What is the effect of smoking on your health:
a if your blood pressure is normal
b if your blood pressure is high?
c How do you explain this difference?

3 Darren says his grandad has always smoked 20 cigarettes a day and he is 80 years old and fit as a fiddle, so smoking can't do you any harm. What would you say to Darren to try and convince him that his argument is not scientifically sound?

Disappointed vampires?

Blood is an amazing liquid. It carries oxygen, carbon dioxide, dissolved food and waste products. It also carries chemical messages which control growth, reproduction and the day-to-day balance of your body. Blood forms clots which dry into scabs when you cut yourself, stopping you from bleeding to death. Blood contains cells which can destroy many disease-causing micro-organisms. If we lose some blood, the body can make more.

In spite of all this, people are trying to produce artificial blood. There is a shortage of blood donors, and blood has to be stored carefully. Some diseases can be passed on through the blood. Some religious groups will not accept blood transfusions, even if it means the difference between life and death. But so far no one has been able to make artificial blood that works as well as the real thing. At the moment, the best that we can manage is a liquid which will transport oxygen and release it to the cells.

4a How could this oxygen-transporting liquid be useful in saving lives?
b What do you think are the problems of making an artificial blood that works like real blood?

Elements and compounds

2a Atoms and molecules

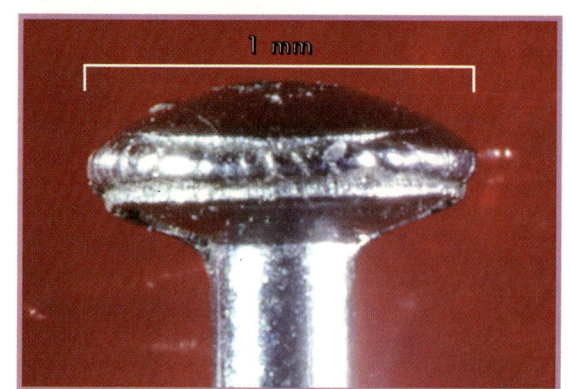

All materials are made of particles that are too small to see, even with a microscope.

a How many particles do you think there are on the head of this pin?

50 thousand? 50 million? 50 thousand million? 50 million million?

  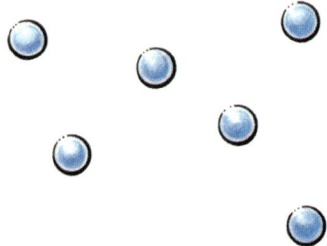

| In solids, the particles are closely packed and stuck together. | In liquids, they are closely packed but free to move. | In gases, they are widely spaced. |

b Use these different arrangements of particles to explain how solids, liquids and gases behave.

Turn up the magnification

In your diagrams, you probably draw particles as little round balls. But imagine you could make them bigger and bigger, so you could see them more clearly. You would find that different particles come in different shapes and sizes.

The large, clumpy-looking particles in the picture are called **molecules**. They are made up of smaller, round particles called **atoms**.

Different molecules are made of different collections of atoms, so they have different shapes.

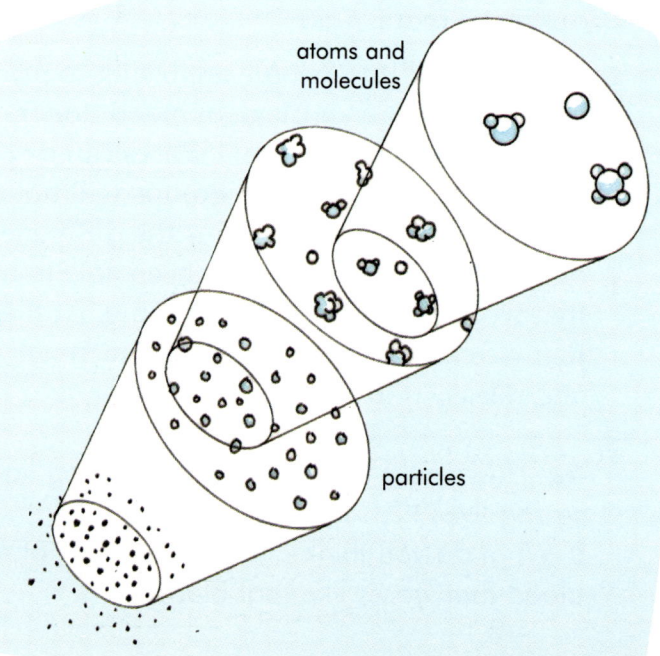

What shape are molecules?

The molecules in any one substance are always the same. Water molecules are made from three atoms. They look rather like the head and ears of a famous cartoon mouse!

Here are the shapes of some other molecules.

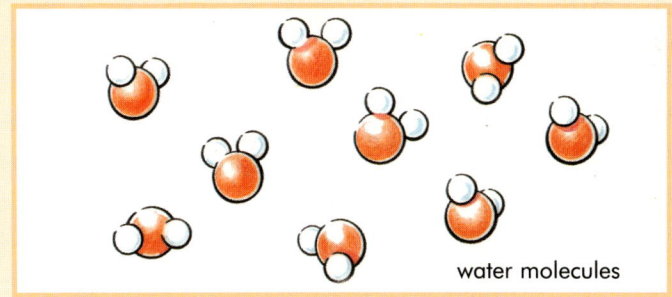
water molecules

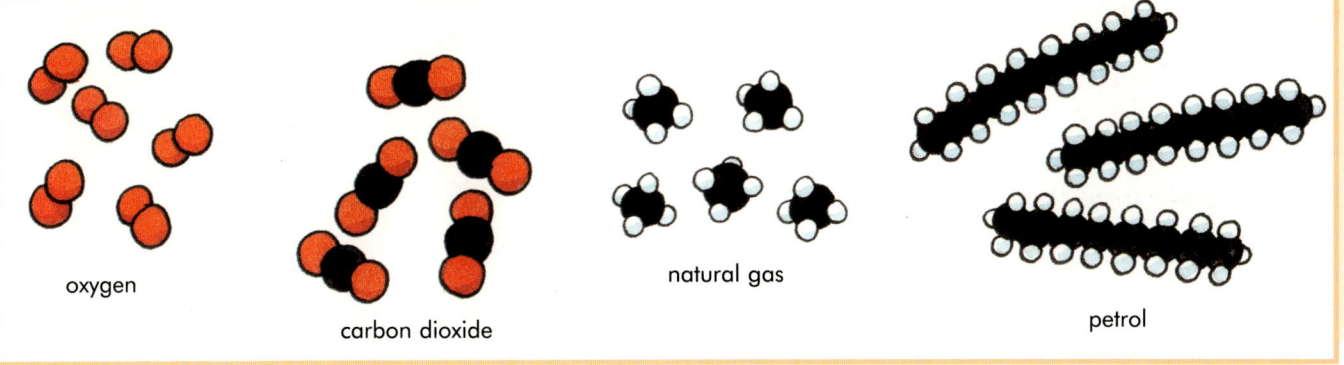

oxygen

carbon dioxide

natural gas

petrol

Breaking up molecules

If you splash some water, you get lots of little droplets of water. If you could break up these little droplets again and again, you would get tinier and tinier droplets of water.

Imagine you could break the tiny droplets up into molecules of water. Now imagine smashing the molecules up into separate atoms. You would no longer have water! The water molecule is the smallest particle of water that you can get. If you break up the water molecule, you change it into different substances.

2 What substance has molecules shaped like this?

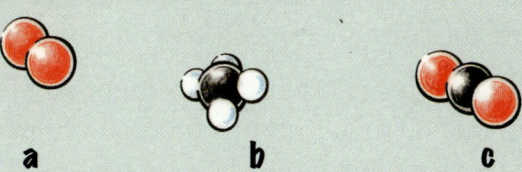

a   b   c

3 What happens to a substance if you break up its molecules?

What do you know?

1 Copy and complete the following sentences. Use the words below to fill the gaps.

| atoms | different | molecule | smaller | same |

The smallest particle in many substances is a _____. All the molecules of one substance are the _____. Different substance have _____ molecules. Molecules are made up of _____ particles called _____.

Key ideas

Many substances are made up of particles called **molecules**.

Different substances have different molecules.

Molecules are made up of smaller particles called **atoms**.

If you break up a molecule, you no longer have the same substance.

23

Elements and compounds

2b The elements

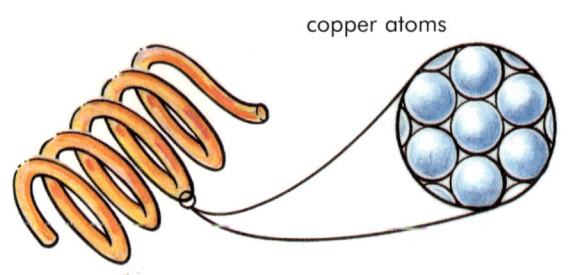

Copper is an element. It has only one type of atom.

What is an element?

In Science, an **element** is a substance that is made of only one kind of atom. As there are 92 different kinds of atoms, there are 92 different elements on Earth. Everything on Earth is made from these 92 elements.

Most elements are solids. Ten elements are gases at room temperature, and only two elements are liquids.

On these two pages we shall look at a few elements.

Mercury

Mercury is unusual, because it is a liquid metal. Mercury is the silver liquid used in some thermometers.

Mercury is mixed with silver (another element) to make the metal fillings for teeth. Mercury can be very poisonous. Hat-makers used to use mercury, and it made some of them go mad. But don't worry if you have fillings in your teeth. Mercury in this form is quite safe, and you won't become 'as mad as a hatter'.

Oxygen

Oxygen is a gas in the air. You need oxygen when you breathe. To make oxygen condense to a liquid, you would have to get it very cold indeed, as its boiling point is −183 °C!

Carbon

Coal, soot, charcoal, and even the 'lead' in your pencil are all made from the element carbon. Carbon is a solid at room temperature. Its melting point is very high, nearly 4000 °C.

Carbon is usually black and soft, but one form of carbon is colourless and very hard indeed.

a What is it? (Hint: look at the photographs.)

Some forms of carbon

Iron

Iron is not usually found as an element on Earth, but sometimes chunks of iron called meteorites crash into the Earth from outer space. These pieces of metal that fell from the sky were highly prized by our ancestors.

Iron is still a very important metal today. It is used for bridges, railways, cars and machinery. More iron is used than all the other metals put together.

This enormous crater in Arizona, USA, formed when an iron meteor crashed into the Earth.

Sulphur

Yellow crystals of sulphur are often found in rocks around volcanoes. Sulphur melts easily but it also catches fire, giving off choking fumes. Since ancient times it has been mixed with carbon and other chemicals to make gunpowder. Today it is used in medicines and pesticides, and for making rubber hard.

Sulphur crystals on a volcano

What do you know?

1 Copy and complete the following sentences. Use the words below to fill the gaps.

| sulphur | 92 | element | atoms |

Everything is made up of _____. There are _____ different kinds of atoms. A substance that is made up of one kind of atom only is called an _____. Carbon, oxygen, _____ and iron are all elements.

2a How many different elements are there on Earth?
b How many of them are solids?

3a Where are you likely to find the element sulphur?
b What was it used to make in the past?

4a What is unusual about the element mercury?
b Why should the mercury from a broken thermometer be cleared up carefully?

Key ideas

All substances are made up of atoms.

There are 92 different kinds of atoms.

A substance made from only one type of atom is called an **element**.

There are 92 different elements on Earth, each with its own type of atoms.

Elements and compounds

2c Mixtures and compounds

Mixing them up

Iron is an element. It is made from iron atoms only, and has its own special properties. It is a grey, magnetic metal.

Sulphur is an element. It is made from sulphur atoms only, and has its own special properties. It is a yellow non-metal.

If you mix iron and sulphur, you mix up the iron and sulphur atoms. But the iron and sulphur still keep their special properties. You just have a **mixture** of iron and sulphur.

a How could you separate the iron from a mixture of iron and sulphur?

Reacting them together

Mixing iron and sulphur is a **physical process**, like dissolving. It is easy to separate them again. But if you heat the mixture with a Bunsen burner, something different happens. The mixture starts to glow, and this glow spreads along the tube.

A **chemical reaction** is taking place. The reaction gives off enough heat to keep itself going. The glow continues even if you turn off the gas.

Something new

When a chemical reaction takes place, a new substance forms. The iron and sulphur combine to make a new substance called iron sulphide. You can write this reaction as a word equation:

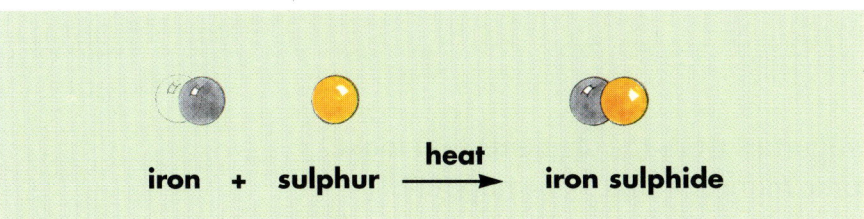

iron + sulphur →(heat) iron sulphide

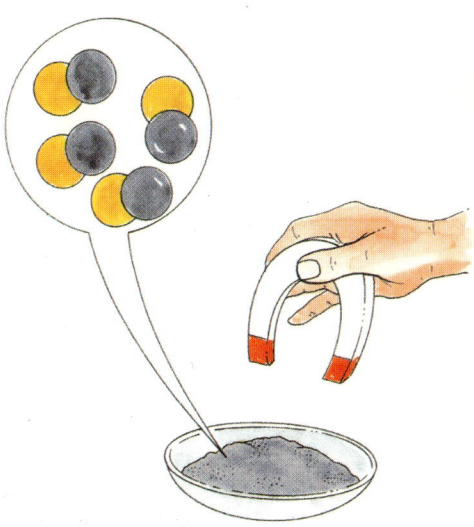

Iron sulphide is a grey solid which is not magnetic. It has different properties from iron and sulphur. The atoms of iron and sulphur have joined together, and made molecules of iron sulphide.

Making a compound

Substances made from two (or more) different atoms chemically joined together are called **compounds**. Each compound has its own properties, which may be very different from the elements it is made from. Iron sulphide is a compound of iron and sulphur.

Molecules in elements

You can get molecules in elements, as well as in compounds. For example, the oxygen in the air has molecules made from two oxygen atoms joined together.

What do you know?

1 How do you know that a chemical reaction takes place when you heat a mixture of iron and sulphur?

2 Look at pictures **A** to **D**, showing different molecules. For each, say whether the picture shows an element, a mixture or a compound.

3 Which of pictures **A** to **D** could represent oxygen?

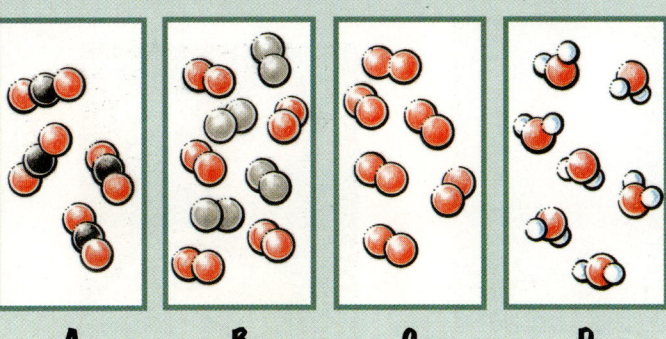

A   B   C   D

Key ideas

If elements are simply mixed together, they keep their individual properties. They can easily be separated.

If elements combine chemically, they form **compounds**. These compounds have new and often quite different properties from the elements.

Elements and compounds

2d More about compounds

Compounds have very different properties from the elements that make them up. These two pages show some more examples of compounds.

Sodium and chlorine

sodium + chlorine → sodium chloride

Sodium is a soft, silvery metal with a very low density. It reacts very strongly with oxygen and water. It has to be stored in oil to stop the air getting to it and to keep it dry.

Chlorine is a green, poisonous gas. It is used to kill germs. Bleach contains chlorine.

Joined together in a compound, these two dangerous elements make sodium chloride. This is the salt you put on your chips!

a 1 From what you know about common salt, try to describe its properties.

2 Compare these properties with those of sodium and chlorine.

Magnesium and oxygen

magnesium + oxygen → magnesium oxide

Magnesium is a silvery metal. It is mixed with aluminium to make metals for aircraft.

Oxygen is the colourless gas in the air that you need to breathe. The air is about one-fifth oxygen.

Magnesium burns in air. It combines with the oxygen to make magnesium oxide. This white powder is used in some indigestion tablets.

28

Carbon, hydrogen and oxygen

Carbon is a black solid element that is found as coal. Hydrogen is a light gaseous element. It used to be used to fill airships, but it was too explosive and caused accidents. By combining carbon, hydrogen and oxygen together in different ways, we get some different compounds.

Natural gas is made from just carbon and hydrogen. Its scientific name is methane.

carbon (solid) + hydrogen (gas) → methane (gas)

Carbon dioxide is produced if you burn carbon in air. It is a compound of carbon and oxygen.

carbon (solid) + oxygen (gas) → carbon dioxide (gas)

Water is made if you burn hydrogen in air. It is a compound of hydrogen and oxygen.

hydrogen (gas) + oxygen (gas) → water (liquid)

▶ b **1** Which substances shown in the photograph are elements and which are compounds?

2 There is oxygen as well. Where is it?

Organic compounds

The three elements carbon, hydrogen and oxygen can combine together in other ways to make an enormous number of very complex compounds. These are sometimes called **organic compounds**. They are the chemicals that make up all living things on Earth – including you!

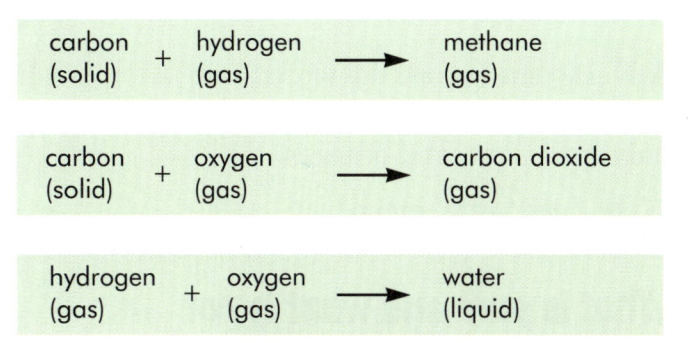

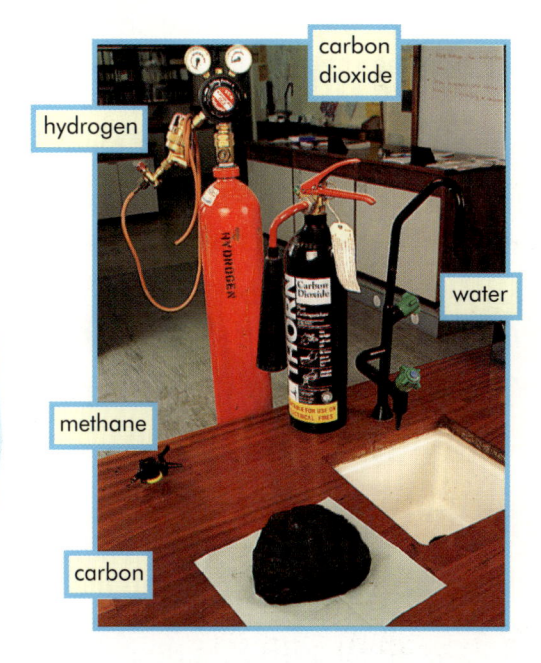

What do you know?

1a Sodium is a metal that floats on water. What is unusual about this?

b Why is sodium stored under oil in a bottle?

2a Why is chlorine gas dangerous?

b How is this property put to good use today?

3 When magnesium burns in air, a white powder forms and a bright white light is given off. Explain how these two clues suggest that a chemical reaction is taking place.

4 What elements are you built from?

Key ideas

When elements combine, a wide range of compounds can be formed.

All living things are made from complex **organic compounds**, formed mostly from carbon, hydrogen and oxygen.

Elements and compounds

2e It's a mixed up world

Advertisements use the word 'pure' a lot. Washing powders will give you pure white sheets. Pure orange juice is made only from squeezed oranges.

a What does 'pure' mean?

What is pure and what is not

Scientists use the word 'pure' in a slightly different way. Orange juice may be made from only oranges, but it is a complex mixture of compounds dissolved in water. Orange juice contains natural sugars, vitamin C and many other substances.

In Science, a **pure** substance contains only one compound or element. All its particles are the same.

Very few common substances are really pure. Almost all natural substances are mixtures of chemicals. It's a mixed up world!

b What particles would a bottle of pure water contain?

Mineral water is not pure. It contains dissolved chemicals.

The air you breathe

The air you breathe is a mixture. About one-fifth of dry air is oxygen. Most of the rest is nitrogen. There are also small amounts of other gases such as carbon dioxide (the gas you breathe out).

The rocks, too

The natural chemical compounds in rocks are called **minerals**. The granite of Dartmoor is a mixture of minerals.

The water you drink

Two-thirds of the Earth's surface is covered by water, but you couldn't drink it! Sea water is a solution, with lots of salt (sodium chloride) and many other substances dissolved in it.

c Is a lungful of fresh mountain air scientifically pure?

granite is a mixture of minerals

Is anything natural pure?

The simple answer is not much! Rainwater in pollution-free areas is almost pure water, but even this contains some dissolved carbon dioxide, oxygen and nitrogen.

White sugar and salt are almost pure substances. Sugar is found mixed up in the sap of sugar cane. Salt is found mixed up with sand and clay in the rocks. Before you use them, they are separated out from their natural mixtures by physical processes such as dissolving, filtration and evaporation.

Natural mixtures are processed to get the pure compound.

How pure is your water?

If you leave sea water to evaporate in a dish, it leaves a thick crust of salt behind. Pure water leaves nothing behind, however.

d. Use this idea to plan an experiment to compare the purity of some different water samples. You could use tap water, rainwater and some different mineral waters.

- How would you compare the results?
- How would you make sure that it was a fair test?

1 Warm some watch-glasses.

2 Put one drop of water on each. (tap water, rainwater)

3 Wait while the water evaporates. (tap water, rainwater)

4 Look carefully and record your results.

Here's a way to speed things up.

What do you know?

1 Copy and complete the following sentences. Use the words below to fill the gaps.

| particles | mixtures | different | pure | same |

If a substance is _____, it contains only one chemical compound, so all its particles are the _____. Most natural substances are _____. They are made up of _____ chemical compounds, with their different _____ all mixed together.

2 Explain why orange juice is not pure in the scientific sense.

3 Draw a pie chart to show the proportions of oxygen and nitrogen in air.

4 What is the difference between the salt you use in cooking and the salt that is dug from the ground?

Key ideas

In Science, a **pure** substance contains just one chemical compound or element.

In a pure substance, all the particles are the same.

In nature, most substances are mixtures.

Elements and compounds

2f More about elements

Oxygen all around

Oxygen is the most common element on Earth. There is some oxygen in the air. But oxygen is very reactive, so most of it is 'locked up' in chemical compounds. For example, sand is made from a compound of oxygen and silicon, called **silica** (silicon dioxide). Water is a compound of hydrogen and oxygen.

a If oxygen is so reactive, why is there some unreacted oxygen in the air?

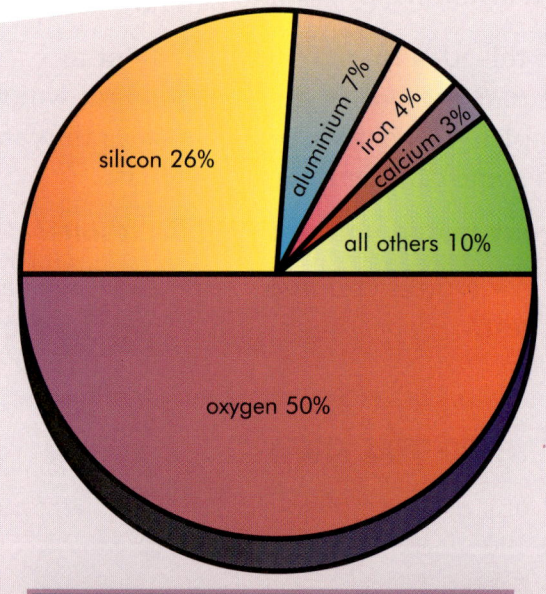

What a lot of oxygen!

Elements in the Earth

There are 92 different elements on Earth. Like oxygen, most of them are 'locked up' in chemical compounds. Some are common, while others are rare. The pie chart shows the percentages of elements in the Earth.

b Five elements make up 90% of the Earth's crust. What are they?

The two most common metals are aluminium and iron. There is lots of aluminium combined with silicon and oxygen in mud. The problem is that the aluminium is so tightly 'locked up' that it costs too much to get it out.

Gold is a very rare element. It makes up just 0.000 000 5% of the Earth's crust. But, if you are very lucky, you could find a pure gold nugget just lying around. Gold is very unreactive, so it is not 'locked up' in compounds. You can find it **uncombined**. That is also why it stays shiny and attractive.

Pie chart: oxygen 50%, silicon 26%, aluminium 7%, iron 4%, calcium 3%, all others 10%

Gold is prized because it is so unreactive.

Metals and non-metals

Seventy of the 92 elements are metals. These are all solids except for mercury. Metals all conduct electricity and heat, and have a shiny metallic appearance.

The remaining 22 elements are non-metals. These generally do not conduct electricity or heat well, and do not have a metallic appearance. Some non-metals, like carbon and sulphur, are solids. Others, like chlorine and oxygen, are gases.

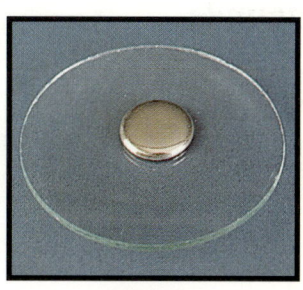

Iron

Chlorine

Mercury

Bromine

Sodium

Silicon

c Which of these are metals and which are non-metals?

A shorthand for elements

We use **symbols** containing one or two letters as a kind of shorthand for the elements. The first letter is always a capital letter. Some symbols are obvious from the name of the element. Others are based on older names for the elements that are no longer used.

Here are a few important symbols to learn.

Metals
- Al — Aluminium
- Zn — Zinc
- Mg — Magnesium
- Ca — Calcium
- Cu — Copper
- Fe — Iron
- Na — Sodium
- Au — Gold
- Ag — Silver
- Pb — Lead

These symbols (Cu, Fe, Na, Au, Ag, Pb) are based on older names that are no longer used.

Non-metals
- H — Hydrogen
- O — Oxygen
- C — Carbon
- S — Sulphur
- Cl — Chlorine
- N — Nitrogen
- Si — Silicon

What do you know?

1a Draw up a table showing the percentages of the different elements in the Earth's crust.
b Draw a bar chart from your table.
2 Why is silica so common in the rocks?
3 Gold is very rare. Explain why you might find a piece of gold in the rocks if you are lucky, but you could never find a piece of pure aluminium.
4 List the properties of metallic and non-metallic elements.

Key ideas

Five elements make up 90% of the Earth's crust.

Only a few elements such as gold are found **uncombined** in nature.

More than three-quarters of all the elements are metals.

Every element has its own **symbol**.

Elements and compounds
2 EXTRAS

2c Air is a mixture

The air is a mixture of atoms and molecules, elements and compounds.

- Nearly 21% of dry air is oxygen. This element forms molecules with two atoms joined together.

- 78% of dry air is nitrogen. This element also forms molecules with two atoms joined together.

- Nearly 1% of dry air is argon. This element exists as single atoms only.

- There is also 0.03% of carbon dioxide. This compound has molecules with one carbon atom joined to two oxygen atoms.

- Air usually contains some water vapour. Water is a compound of hydrogen and oxygen. Its molecules have two tiny hydrogen atoms joined to a larger oxygen atom.

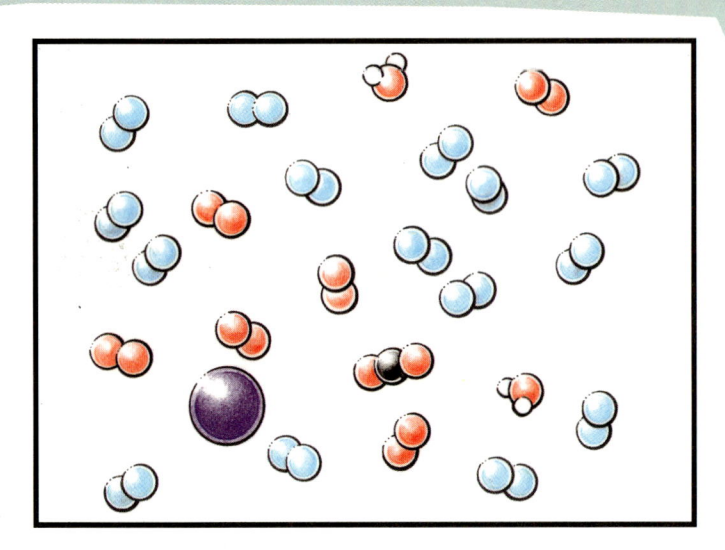

1 Look carefully at this picture. It shows the different particles present in air. Copy one example of each different particle, and answer the following questions for each one:

a What is its name?
b Give a reason for your answer to **a**.
c Is it an element or a compound?
d Is the particle an atom or a molecule?

2d Big molecules

Some molecules can be enormous, with tens, hundreds or even thousands of atoms joined together.

Carbon is an atom that naturally makes big molecules. The carbon atoms can join together to form long chains or branches. All living things are made up of molecules like this.

Scientists have found ways to make big molecules artificially, by joining lots of little molecules together. Chemicals with big molecules like this are called **polymers**. You probably know them better as plastics, such as polythene, polystyrene or PVC.

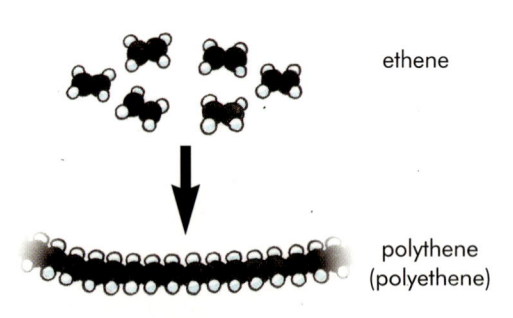

ethene

polythene (polyethene)

1 Polythene is made from ethene. What small molecules do you think the following plastics are made from?

a polystyrene
b polypropylene
c PVC (polyvinylchloride)

2e How pure is 'pure'?

Purifying substances can be difficult and expensive. Things are only purified as much as they need to be to work properly. How pure a substance needs to be depends on the substance, what it is being used for, and what the impurities are.

Beach sand may be 95% silica, which is fine to mix with cement. But much purer sand is needed to make glass, as impurities colour the glass or make it cloudy.

Watermelons are 95% water. They quench your thirst on a hot day, and the remaining 5% is food! Sea water is 96.5% water, but the dissolved salt means it's not good to drink.

1 Table salt is mostly sodium chloride. Most table salt is made from purified rock salt, but some brands are made from sea water.

a Look at the two packets of table salt. What other information would you need before you could decide which was better value?
b Which is better value if both packets contain 250 g of salt?
c Try to find out why some people prefer to buy sea salt.

2f Why oxygen?

In general, the only elements that are found uncombined on Earth are the unreactive metals such as gold and the unreactive gases such as argon. But oxygen is a very reactive element that combines easily to form compounds. Why does it exist as an element in the air?

It's all because of plants! Plants make their own food from simple chemicals using the energy from sunlight. This process is called photosynthesis. Oxygen is made as a by-product in this reaction. Over millions of years of plant life, oxygen built up in the atmosphere. Without plants, all the oxygen in the air would eventually become locked up in stable compounds.

1 If carbon and oxygen were left to react together, what compound would form?

2 What is the energy source that has upset this chemical balance?

3 The oxygen level in the air is no longer increasing. What part do you play in this?

Magnets

3a Attracting and repelling

Magnets are useful things. This fridge door has two magnets. One is stuck to the outside of the fridge. It is useful for holding messages and shopping lists. The other magnet is inside the door. It keeps the door shut when you push it.

a Where else are magnets useful at home?

Bar magnets

A bar magnet is usually made of steel. Its ends are different from each other. One end has a mark or a different colour to show that it is the magnet's north pole. The other end is the magnet's south pole.

You can investigate two magnets by holding them close together. There is a force between them. You can feel this force pushing them apart or pulling them together. The closer together they are, the stronger the force gets.

Pushing apart is called **repelling**. Pulling together is called **attracting**.

Here are the results of an experiment with bar magnets:

Arrangement of magnets	Force between magnets
N N	pushing apart (repelling)
N S	pulling together (attracting)
S S	pushing apart (repelling)

You can see that two different poles (a north pole and a south pole) attract each other, but two poles the same repel each other. People often remember this by saying:

- "Unlike poles attract, like poles repel," or
- "Opposites attract."

36

b 1 You can make a shape with magnets like this. Explain why the magnets will not stick together this way.

2 Draw a square of magnets that will stick together.

Magnetic materials

Magnets can attract each other. They can also attract some other materials. We call these **magnetic materials**.

Iron and steel are magnetic materials. They are metals. But not all metals are magnetic. Copper, aluminium and tin are not magnetic.

Many non-metals are not magnetic either. Wood, water, plastic and glass are not magnetic.

The fridge door in the photograph on the opposite page is made of steel. The steel is covered with white paint. The paint is not a magnetic material. The magnetic force of the magnet can attract the steel through the paint.

c Jenny was testing different materials to see if they are magnetic. She found a surprising result. Can you explain it?

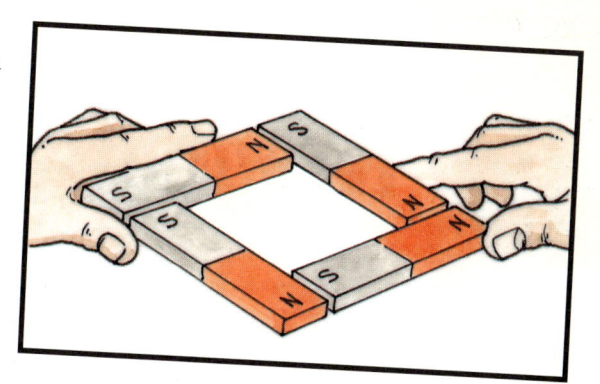

What do you know?

1 Copy these magnets and the sentences beneath them. Complete the sentences, using the words below to fill the gaps. You can use words more than once.

| like | unlike | attract | repel |

These magnets will _____ each other because _____ poles _____.

These magnets will _____ each other because _____ poles _____.

2a Name two magnetic metals.
b Name two metals that are not magnetic.
c Name two non-metals that are not magnetic.

3 Some 2p coins are magnetic, and others are not. Design a machine for automatically sorting out the two kinds of 2p coin.

Key ideas

Magnets **attract** and **repel** one another. Unlike poles attract, like poles repel.

Some metals such as iron and steel, and some other materials, are attracted by magnets. These are called **magnetic materials**.

Magnets

3b Magnetic fields

Magnets can attract and repel each other when they are quite a long way apart. They do not have to be touching.

a Look at the magnets in the pictures. Which magnets are attracting each other? Which are repelling each other? How can you tell?

A field with no grass

There is a **magnetic field** all around a magnet. If you put another magnet in this field, it will be attracted or repelled. If you put a piece of magnetic material in the field, it will be attracted.

You can detect the field around a magnet using iron filings. You put the magnet under a piece of card. You sprinkle iron filings on the card. If you tap the card, the filings move a little. They line up to show the magnetic field.

The magnetic field is strongest near the poles of the magnet. You can see this because the iron filings cluster together near the poles. The field is weaker at the sides of the magnet.

Iron filings can also show the field around two magnets. From the pattern, you can tell whether they are attracting or repelling each other.

b Which photograph shows the magnetic field around two magnets that are attracting each other? Which shows the pattern for two magnets repelling each other?

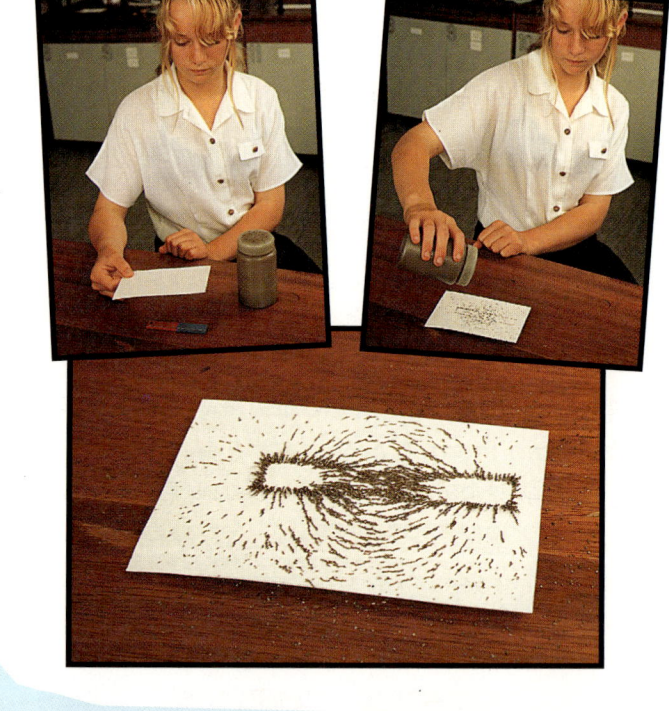

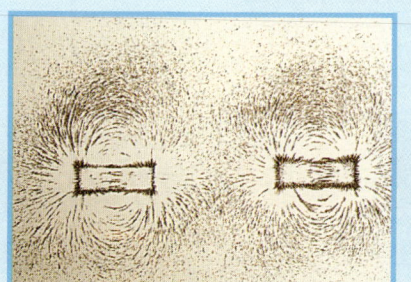

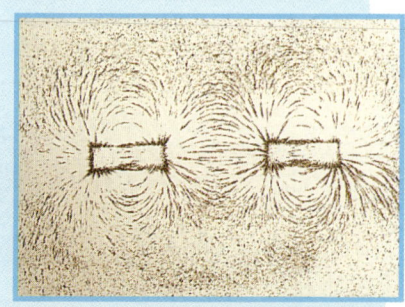

Drawing a field pattern

It is difficult to draw iron filings to show the magnetic field pattern of a magnet. Instead, we draw **lines of force** around the magnet. The arrows come out of the north pole and go into the south pole.

c Copy this diagram showing the magnetic field pattern around a bar magnet. Write the word 'strong' where you think the field is strong. Write the word 'weak' where you think it is weak.

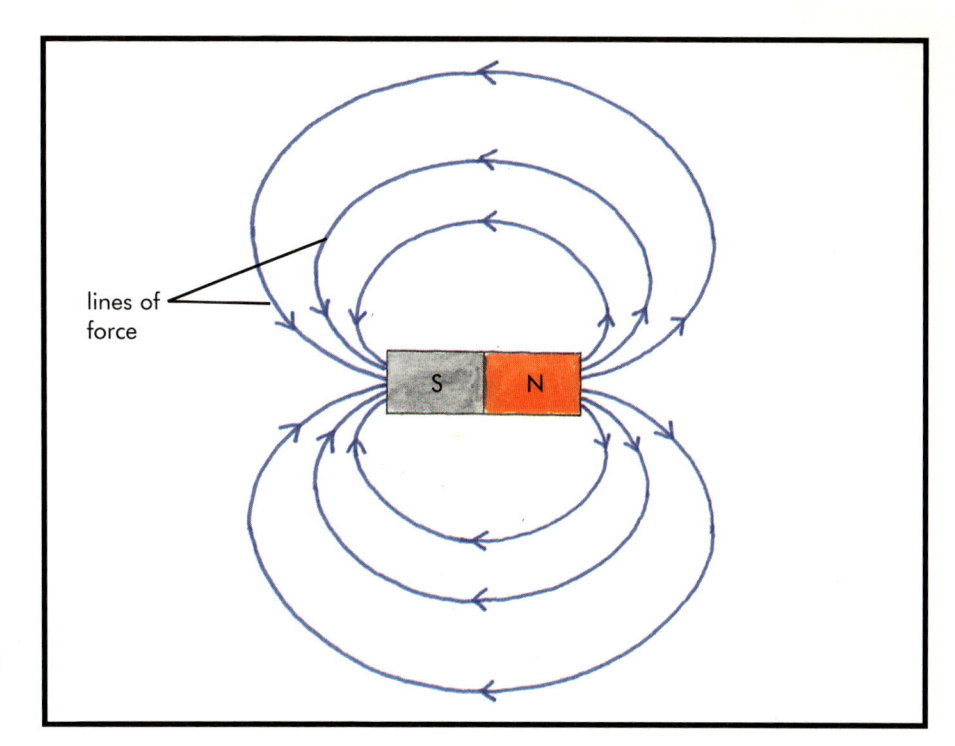

What do you know?

1 Copy and complete the following sentences. Choose the correct word from each pair.

Around every magnet there is a magnetic **field/meadow**. Here, a piece of magnetic material will feel **attracted/repelled**. The field is strongest near the magnet's **sides/poles**. We draw lines of **energy/force** to show the field.

2 These diagrams show the magnetic field patterns around two bar magnets. Which magnet is stronger, **A** or **B**? Give a reason for your answer.

3 This toy uses iron filings. You can give the face a funny hairstyle, or a beard.
a How would you move the iron filings around?
b Why would aluminium filings be no good for this toy?

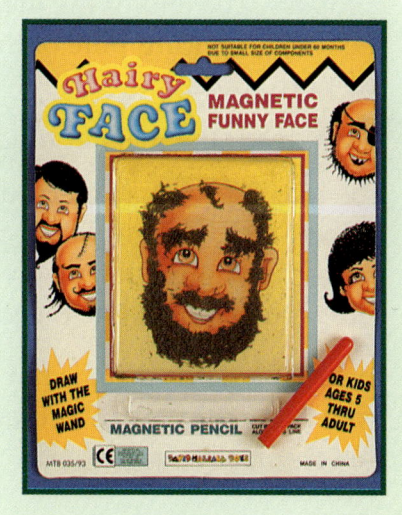

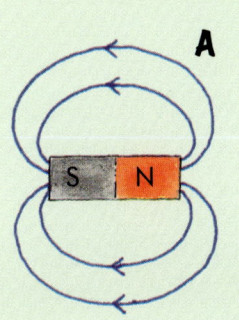

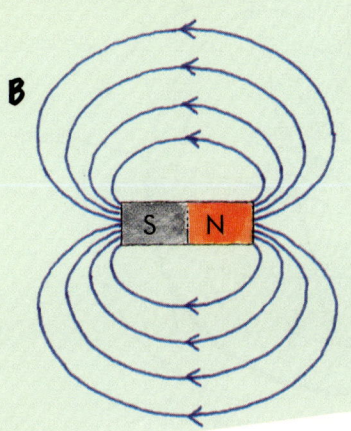

Key ideas

There is a **magnetic field** around a magnet.

We can see the magnetic field pattern using iron filings.

We draw **lines of force** to show the magnetic field.

Magnets

3c The Earth's field

A magnetic **compass** helps you find your way. It helps you work out where you are on the map. One end of the compass needle points towards the Earth's North Pole.

a
1 Who might find a compass useful in their work?
2 Who might find a compass useful in their spare time?

North and south

If you hang a magnet on a string, it will turn around and one end will point to the north. It is like the needle of a compass. The end of the magnet that points north is called the **north-seeking pole** of the magnet, usually shortened to the north pole.

If you push the magnet round gently, it will swing back again.

The magnet is attracted by the Earth's magnetic field. The inside of the Earth behaves like a giant magnet. We can show the pattern of the Earth's magnetic field by drawing lines of force. The pattern is just like the pattern for a bar magnet.

b Inside the Earth there is hot liquid rock which contains a lot of iron. This is the Earth's core. How do you think scientists know that it contains iron?

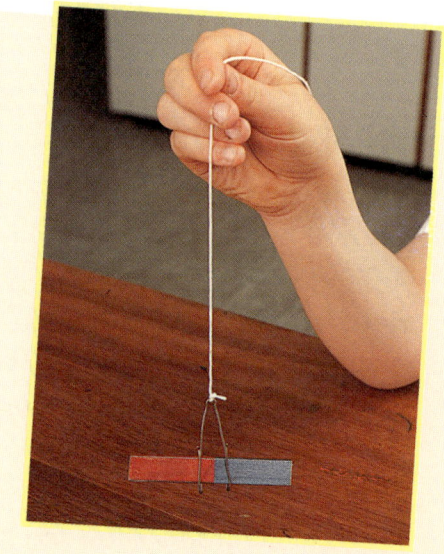

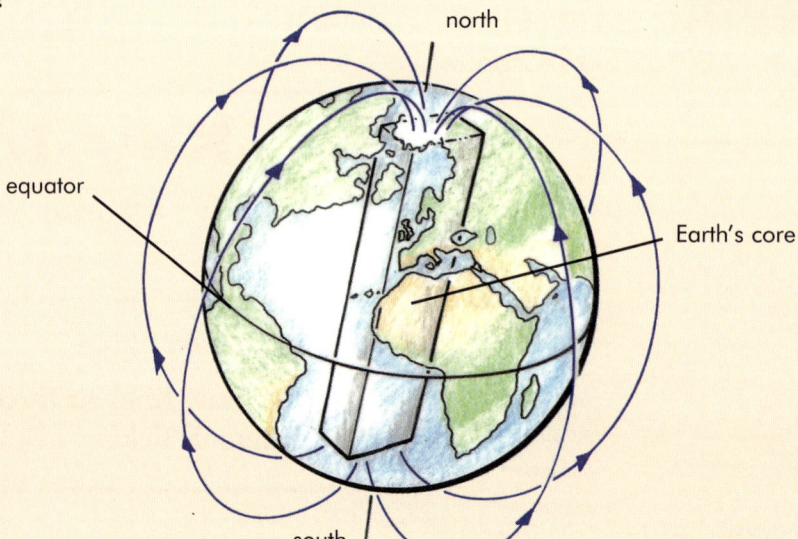

Going home

Racing pigeons can find their way home from hundreds of miles away. They can detect the Earth's magnetic field. They have tiny particles of iron in their heads, like tiny compasses.

Scientists fixed magnets on to a pigeon's head. It did not know which way to fly. They had to rescue it!

c Why could the pigeon not decide which way to fly when it had magnets attached to its head?

Magnetic rocks

If you go out in the mountains, your compass may point the wrong way, because some mountains are made of magnetic rocks. This helps geologists to find iron.

d Why might it be dangerous if your compass pointed the wrong way in the mountains?

Nowadays, a satellite orbiting the Earth can measure the Earth's magnetic field very accurately. The field is especially strong where the rocks contain iron or nickel or other magnetic metals. Geologists can go there to collect some samples for testing.

What do you know?

1 Jane made a compass. She stuck a bar magnet on top of a flat cork, and floated it in a dish of water.
a In which direction will the north pole of the magnet point?
b Why did Jane float the cork in the water?

2a Why is a compass useful for a sailor crossing the Atlantic Ocean?
b How could the sailor find the direction of north or south, without the help of a compass?

Key ideas

The Earth has a magnetic field round it.

The inside of the Earth behaves like a giant magnet.

We use a **compass** to detect the Earth's magnetic field, to help us find our way around.

Magnets

3d Electromagnets

This crane can pick up heavy loads of scrap metal using a magnet. The crane moves the metal above the right pile of scrap, and then the operator switches off the magnet. The metal drops off the crane.

This magnet works using electric current. It is called an **electromagnet**.

a Why is it useful to have a magnet you can switch on and off like this at a scrapyard?

Coils, current and core

To make an electromagnet, you need a coil of wire. You connect the wire up to a power supply, and an electric current flows through it. The coil will attract metal objects such as steel pins.

To make an electromagnet stronger, it needs an iron core. The coil of wire is wound around an iron nail. Then the electromagnet will pick up more pins.

A switch in the circuit means that the electromagnet can be switched on and off.

b Draw a circuit diagram to show how the power supply, switch and electromagnet should be connected together.

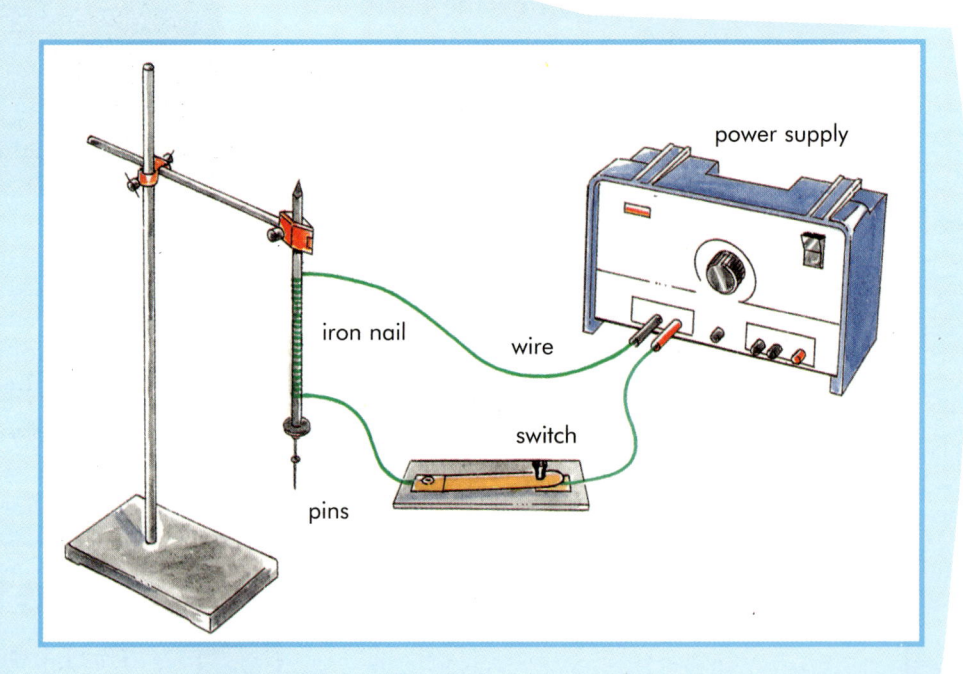

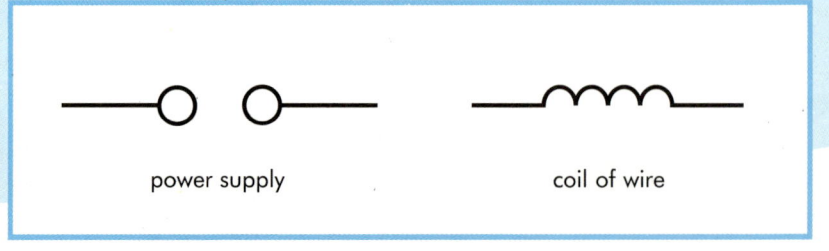

Circuit symbols

42

A stronger electromagnet

An iron core makes an electromagnet stronger, because iron is a magnetic material. There are two other ways to make an electromagnet stronger:

- use a coil with more turns of wire
- use a bigger electric current.

Investigating the magnetic field

You can use iron filings or little compasses called plotting compasses to investigate the magnetic field around an electromagnet. The iron filings show that an electromagnet has a magnetic field just like that around a bar magnet. One end is the north pole, the other end is the south pole.

1 How could you use a compass to help you decide which end is the north pole of the electromagnet?

2 What do you think would happen if you changed round the connections to the power supply, so that the current flows the other way in the coil?

What do you know?

1 Write down three ways to make an electromagnet stronger.

2a Which of these three electromagnets is the strongest? Give a reason for your answer.
b How could you make it even stronger?

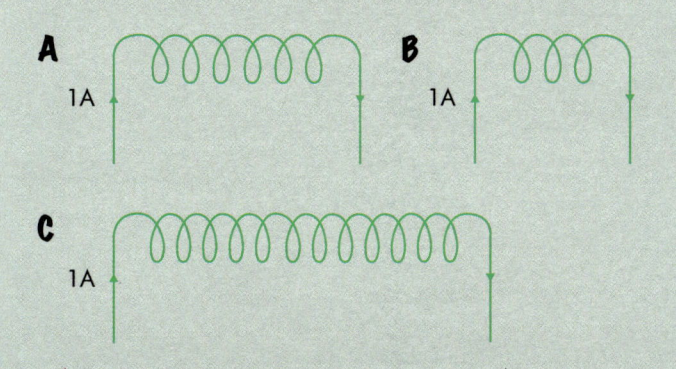

A 1A
B 1A
C 1A

3 Why is an electromagnet sometimes more useful than an ordinary bar magnet?

Key ideas

We can make an **electromagnet** using a coil of wire. When an electric current flows through the coil, it becomes magnetic.

You can make an electromagnet stronger by:

- adding an iron core
- having more turns of wire on the coil
- increasing the current.

There is a magnetic field around an electromagnet, just like the field around a bar magnet.

Magnets

3e Using electromagnets

Electromagnets have many different uses. This surgeon is using an electromagnet to remove steel splinters from someone's eye. He can change the pulling force of the electromagnet by turning a knob.

a How does turning the knob make the electromagnet stronger or weaker?

Open sesame!

Some people have an electromagnetic bolt on their front door. When they want to let you in, they press a switch. The electromagnet pulls back the bolt so that you can open the door.

Once the door is closed behind you, the electromagnet is switched off. The spring pushes the bolt back to lock the door.

b Who would find an electromagnetic bolt like this useful?

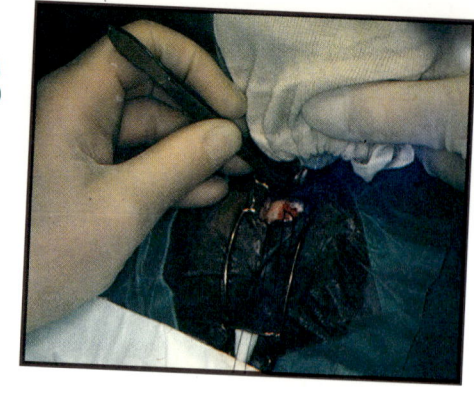

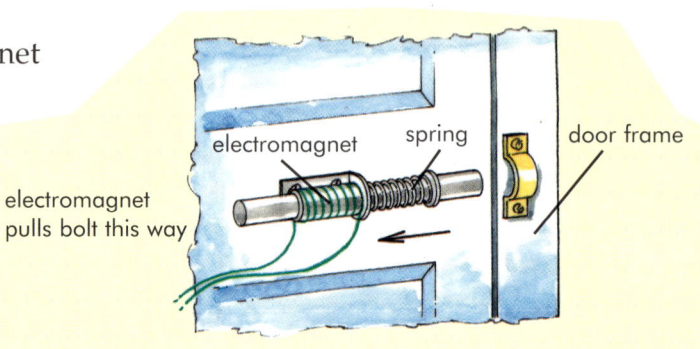

Sending messages

You can send messages in code using an electromagnet. When you close the switch, the magnet attracts the springy metal. The metal hits the magnet with a click. When you open the switch again, the magnet stops working and the metal springs back.

Telegraph messages were sent like this in the nineteenth century. The telegraph operator used Morse code, and the messages could be sent over hundreds of miles.

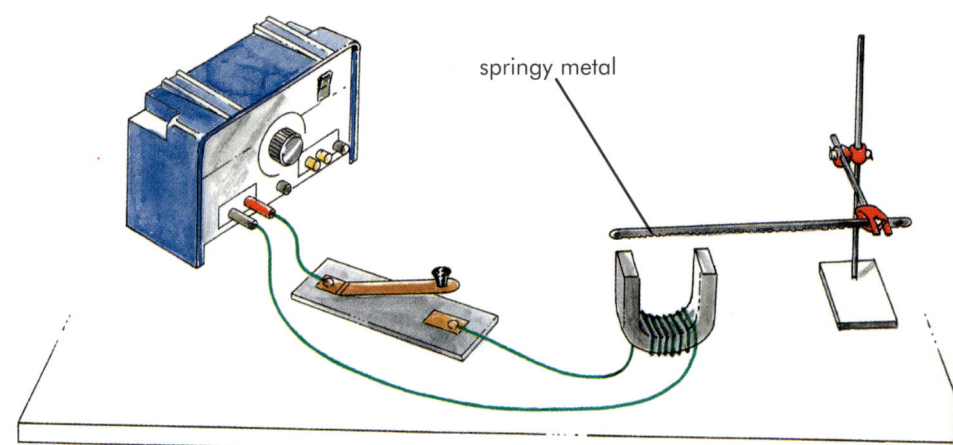

44

Ringing the bell

This electric doorbell uses electromagnets. When you push the switch by the door, the electromagnet attracts the springy metal so that the hammer strikes the gong.

Calling the lift

When you press the button to call a lift, an electric current flows through an electromagnet. This switches on the lift's motor. An electromagnetic switch like this is called a **relay**.

Many other appliances use electromagnets, including motors, dynamos, loudspeakers and television sets. You can't always see the electromagnet from the outside.

C Make a list of things you have with electromagnets in them to make them work.

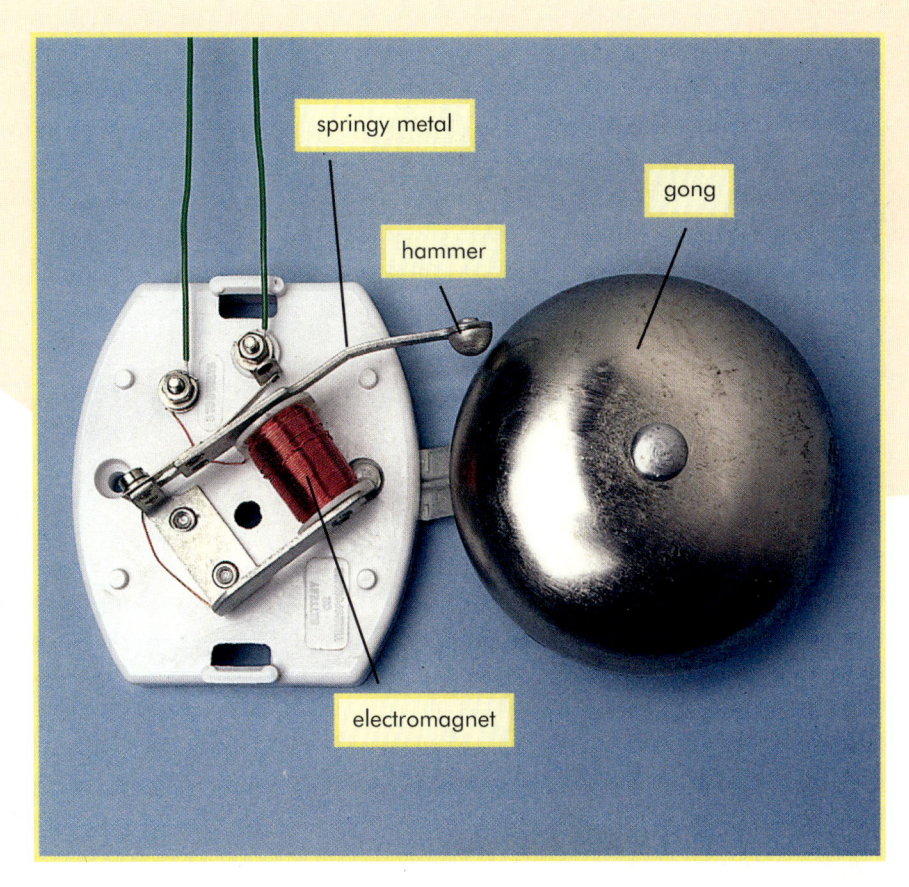

What do you know?

1 Write these sentences in the correct order to explain how the Morse code telegraph on the opposite page works.

- A current flows through the coil.
- The metal clicks against the coil.
- The coil attracts the springy metal.
- The coil becomes magnetic.
- You close the switch.

2 Divide the appliances below into two lists under these headings:

Appliances that use electromagnets and **Appliances that don't use electromagnets**.

electric bell   compass   loudspeaker
light bulb   personal stereo   electric motor

Key ideas

Electromagnets are used in many devices, including buzzers, bells, relays and motors.

Magnets

3 EXTRAS

3b More magnetic field patterns

We can draw lines of force to show the magnetic field patterns when two magnets are placed next to each other.

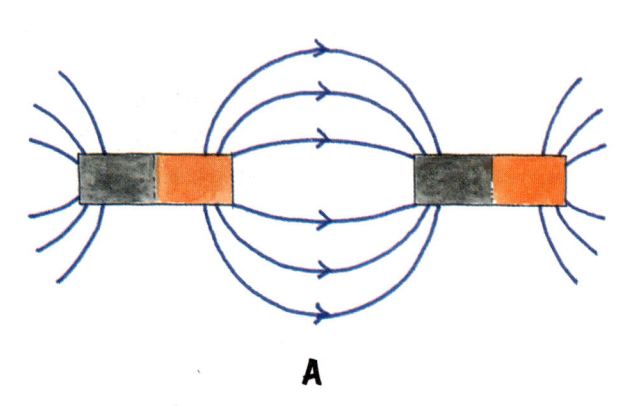

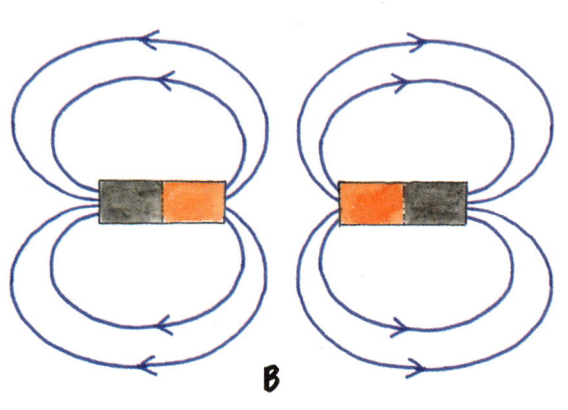

A

B

1a Which of the drawings above shows the pattern for two magnets attracting each other?

b What does the other drawing show?

2 Copy this drawing of two magnets side by side, and add lines of force to show the magnetic field pattern you would expect to find.

3c Compass puzzles

The picture of the Earth on page 40 will help you to answer these questions.

1 Which way will a compass point if you are somewhere south of the equator, for example in South Africa?

2 Which way will a compass point if you are on the equator?

3 Which way will a compass point if you are standing at the North Pole?

3d Investigating an electromagnet

Katie is testing her electromagnet. It is lying on the bench next to a compass. The compass points north before the electromagnet is switched on. Answer the following questions to predict the results of Katie's investigation.

1 What will happen when Katie switches on the power supply?

2 Katie swops over the connections to the power supply. What will happen now when she switches it on?

3 Katie scatters iron filings around the electromagnet. Draw the pattern of lines of force you would expect Katie to observe. Label the north and south poles of the electromagnet.

3e Electric bell

An electric bell is a clever invention. When you press the button, the hammer vibrates back and forth, hitting the gong. It doesn't just hit it once.

1 Write these sentences in the correct order to explain how the bell works.

- You press the button.
- The hammer hits the gong.
- The coils are no longer magnetic.
- The coils become magnetic.
- An electric current flows through the coils.
- The electric circuit is broken.
- The springy metal is attracted to the coils.
- The current stops flowing.
- The circuit is complete again.
- The springy metal springs back.

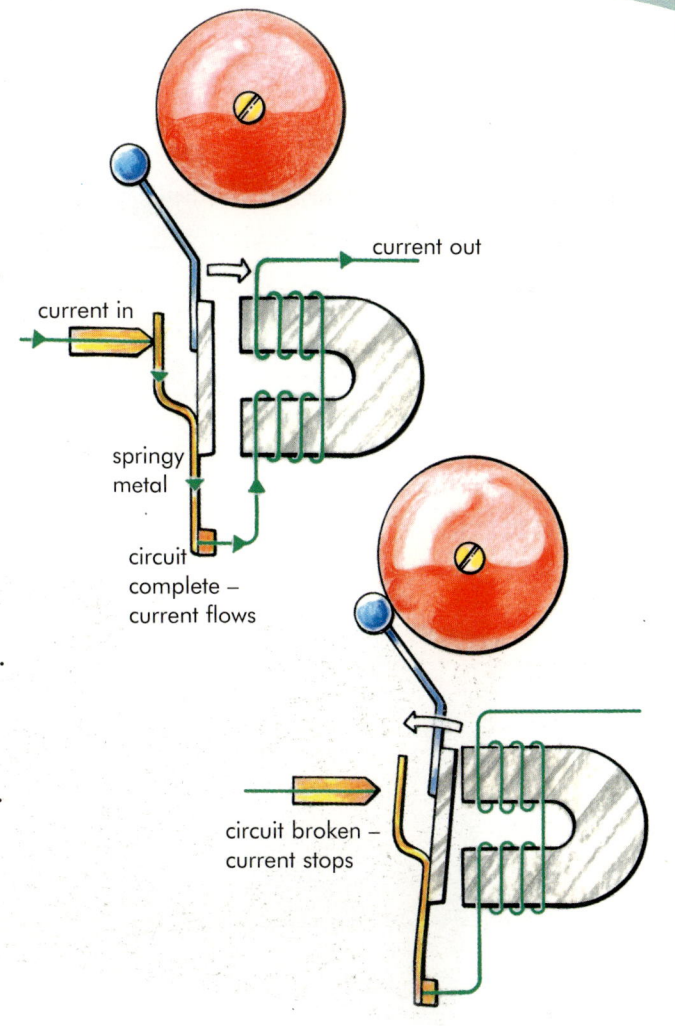

Adaptation

4a Home sweet home

The planet Earth is home to millions of different types or **species** of animals and plants. Looking at the Earth from thousands of miles up in space, we can see that the surface of the planet is not the same all over. There are lots and lots of different kinds of places for different organisms to live in. The place where an animal or plant lives is called its **habitat**.

a Write down all the different sorts of habitats you can think of.

At home in the garden

These pictures show some very different habitats. But different habitats don't have to be far apart. In a single garden there may be lots of different habitats.

b Write down all the different sorts of garden habitats you can think of.

Different habitats are usually home to very different types of animals and plants. The picture shows the organisms living in some garden habitats.

Each organism needs a different sort of habitat. Dragonflies and slugs couldn't live on the hot sunny flowerbed, and greenfly don't live on grass.

Living together

All the animals and plants living in a particular area are part of the same **ecosystem**. Things like the type of soil and the weather affecting the animals and plants are also part of the ecosystem. Animals and plants all need a habitat which suits them. They live in balance with the other organisms around them in their ecosystem.

The damp area around a pond is home to mosses and ferns, water beetles and dragonflies, frogs, fish and slugs.

A south-facing sunny flowerbed is home to bright flowering plants, ladybirds and greenfly.

A lawn is home to beetles and worms, mosses and a few tough plants like daisies and dandelions.

What do you know?

1 Copy and complete the following sentences. Use the words below to fill the gaps.

> Arctic   soil   desert   habitat
> ecosystem   weather

The place where a plant or animal lives is its _____. Habitats range from the ice of the _____ to the dry heat of the _____. An _____ is both the living organisms in an area and things like the _____ and _____ which affect them.

2 Desert animals cannot cope with very cold conditions, and animals and plants from cold climates don't thrive in hot places. Human beings can live in most of the Earth's habitats. How do we manage this?

3 Think about your school and its surroundings. Describe three different habitats along with the sort of living things you might find there.

Key ideas

The **habitat** of an animal or plant is the place where it lives.

Different habitats support different plants and animals.

An **ecosystem** is all the animals and plants living in an area, along with things like the soil and weather which affect them.

Adaptation

4b Round pegs in round holes

Most animals and plants are **adapted** to the ecosystem they live in. This means they are well suited to the place where they live. By looking at an animal or plant, we can get a good idea of where and how it lives.

Surviving

Animals and plants go to great lengths to survive different conditions. Some have developed fantastic ways to overcome the problems of survival. Here are some of the ways animals are adapted to their particular ways of life.

The long neck of the giraffe allows it to feed on the leaves from the tops of trees that no other animals can reach.

The habitat of the Venus fly trap has soil containing very few minerals. The leaves of the plant are adapted to catch and digest insects. The minerals the plant needs come from the insects.

The plaice can change colour to merge into the background. This is called **camouflage**. This hides it from other fish which would eat it.

Fact files

The barn owl has:
- excellent hearing
- large eyes
- a sharp beak and claws
- light bones and feathers.

The cheetah has:
- very small ears
- spotted fur
- sharp pointed teeth
- very long legs.

The rabbit has:
- long ears
- large eyes
- strong hind legs
- flat grinding teeth.

The cactus has:
- a thick stem with lots of water-storing cells
- tiny spines as leaves
- a waxy outer layer
- very deep roots.

a Look at the fact files and write about how these organisms are adapted to their ecosystem.

What do you know?

1 Copy and complete the following sentences.
a The _____ has a long neck to reach the leaves at the tops of trees.
b The _____ is a plant which survives in the desert by storing water in its stem and having spines for leaves.
c The spots of a _____ help to camouflage it as it hunts.
d An _____ is a bird with big eyes for seeing at night, sharp claws and a very light skeleton.

2 Think of four habitats. Write down one organism from each one. Make a fact file to show how each organism is suited to its ecosystem.

Key ideas

Animals and plants are **adapted** to suit their ecosystem and their way of life.

The whole organism, parts of the organism or the outer covering may be adapted.

Adaptation

4c All change

Animals and plants have to be adapted to their environment at all times. In some parts of the world, near the equator, the weather is very similar all year round. But in lots of other places it changes enormously through the year.

a Think of the four seasons in Britain. Write down the different conditions that living organisms have to cope with in one year.

The bare necessities

In the middle of summer, a tree like this is getting about 16 hours of sunlight each day and the average temperature will be around 20 °C. In these conditions plenty of photosynthesis can take place. This supplies the tree with food for growing and making flowers, fruits and seeds.

But in the middle of winter, the average temperature is 5 °C and daylight lasts for only 8 hours. There isn't enough sunlight for the leaves to make much food by photosynthesis, and they would all be killed by the frost. So the tree becomes **dormant**. It loses its leaves and slows down all the processes of life. It can survive until the warmer weather and longer days of spring.

Changing with the seasons

Many other plants avoid the short, cold days of winter by becoming dormant. They may survive as seeds, or as bulbs under the ground. They may have specially adapted leaves which mean they can survive the worst conditions. Animals have to survive these changes too. Some animals change their behaviour. Some change the way they look, and others change the way their bodies work.

b Make a list of some of the ways animals cope with seasonal changes.

Dormice and other animals **hibernate** in cold weather. They eat a lot and build up fat stores first. Their bodies slow down to save energy. They become active again when the days get longer and warmer.

In the winter, ponies have thick shaggy coats which keep them warm. In the warmer days of spring, the shaggy coat falls out leaving a shorter, thinner coat for the summer. Lots of animals are adapted like this to cope with temperature changes.

Colours of change

Animals often change colour, as well as the amount of fur they have, to help them survive. If your colouring hides you from your **predators** or **prey** in the summer, you will easily be seen in the winter snow. So lots of animals adapt for the change in seasons with a change in colouring.

arctic hare

arctic fox

The arctic fox and the arctic hare adapt to the winter snow by developing thick white winter coats.

What do you know?

1 Copy and complete the following sentences. Use the words below to fill the gaps.

| leaves | hibernate | dormant |
| summer | seasons | cold |

In Britain there are four _____ in the year. In _____ it is warm and there are long hours of sunlight. In winter it is _____ and the days are short. Many trees produce _____ in the spring, then lose them and become _____ during the winter. Animals like the dormouse _____ when the cold weather comes.

2a Why do New Forest ponies grow thick shaggy coats in the autumn?
b Why do arctic foxes change from blue-grey to white in winter?

3 Before a dormouse hibernates, it:
a builds up as much body fat as possible
b finds a small place to hide in and fills it with dried grass and leaves.
c When the dormouse hibernates, all its body processes slow right down. The heart rate and breathing are so slow the animal seems dead.
Explain how each of these things helps the dormouse to survive the winter.

Key ideas

Animals and plants need to survive seasonal changes in their habitat.

Plants may become **dormant** and animals **hibernate** to avoid difficult conditions.

Mammals often change the amount and colour of their fur with the seasons.

Adaptation

4d Chains, pyramids and biomass

The plants and animals that live in similar habitats are linked by food chains. This simple food chain tells us that rabbits eat grass, and foxes eat rabbits. It doesn't tell us how many rabbits there are, or how many foxes.

a **1** How many rabbits do you think a fox eats in a week?

2 How many blades of grass do you think that number of rabbits would eat in a week?

grass ⟶ rabbit ⟶ fox

Building a pyramid of numbers

Thousands of grass plants will feed only a small number of rabbits. These rabbits will feed only one fox. If we know the numbers of organisms in a food chain, we can arrange them in a **pyramid of numbers**.

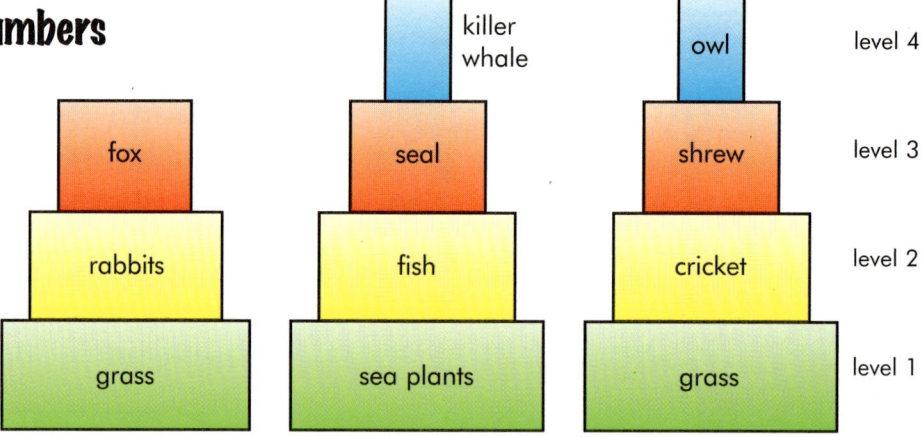

level 4	killer whale	owl
level 3	fox / seal	shrew
level 2	rabbits / fish	cricket
level 1	grass / sea plants	grass

Plants are **producers**, because they produce their own food by photosynthesis. Animals **consume** plants or other animals. There are many more producers than consumers. The numbers of consumers fall as you go up the pyramid.

b What do you think is the reason for this?

c Write down three more food chains and then sketch pyramids of numbers for them. They may not all fall into the same pattern.

54

A rose bush pyramid

Rose bushes are often attacked by greenfly. The greenfly are eaten by ladybirds. The food chain looks easy.

But the pyramid of numbers looks rather odd! One large plant is supporting lots of tiny animals. You often get strange pyramids of numbers like this.

rose bush ⟶ greenfly ⟶ ladybirds

ladybirds
greenfly
rose

Biomass

When an animal eats a plant, not all the food in the plant ends up as new living material in the animal. The food gets used for other things.

When the animal is eaten itself, it passes along only the food that has become part of its body. The next organism gets only the small amount of food that was turned into new biological material. This biological material is called **biomass**.

Some food is used for respiration. This provides energy for the animal to move about, excrete and reproduce.

A small amount of the food eaten is used by the animal to grow. It becomes part of the animal's body.

Energy from respired food is used by birds and mammals to keep warm.

Some of the food passes out of the body as undigested waste.

What do you know?

1 Write out these sentences, putting the correct pairs together.

Food chains link plants and animals	a pyramid of numbers.
Only food that is turned into biomass	living in similar habitats.
By looking at the numbers of organisms in a food chain we can arrange them in	which in turn feed one fox.
Lots of grass plants support a few rabbits	is passed along a food chain.

2 Why is the bottom level of a pyramid of numbers always filled with plants?

3 Design a poster for the lab wall called 'Pyramids in the living world'. Use your poster to explain the links between organisms in food chains.

Key ideas

Pyramids of numbers show the numbers of organisms at each level of a food chain.

Biomass is the amount of biological material in an organism.

Adaptation

4e Helping and hindering

When we grow animals for food, we **manage** a food chain. When we manage a wood to get timber, we alter the food webs there. When we empty our sewage into the sea, we affect the animals and plants there too.

Planting marram grass, which has lots of roots, helps to bind the sand together. This stops the sand dunes blowing away.

a Think of three ways in which people have a good effect on their ecosystem, and three ways in which we do harm.

We sometimes put chemicals into rivers without knowing what they will do to the food webs there. When things go wrong, it is often the bigger fish that suffer most.

The sad story of DDT

DDT is a very powerful chemical which kills insects. It is called a **pesticide**. It kills the insect pests that destroy crops. Unfortunately, it also has a tragic effect on wildlife. DDT does not break down in the bodies of animals. It is simply stored in their fat. In the 1960s, not long after farmers started using DDT in this country, lots of herons died.

b Look at the food chain. Why do you think the herons died? Write down your ideas, then read on to see if you are right.

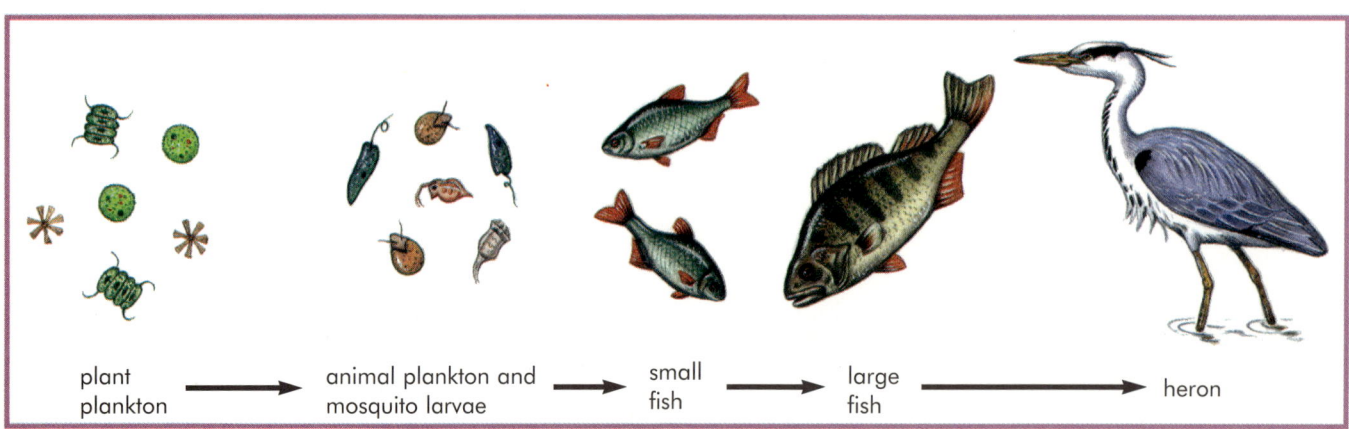

plant plankton → animal plankton and mosquito larvae → small fish → large fish → heron

56

DDT was sprayed onto fields. It got washed into streams and rivers by the rain. It got into the bodies of the tiny animals in the water. They took in such small amounts of DDT that they were not harmed.

Each small fish eats lots of tiny animals. All the DDT stays in the fish's body. The fish has slightly more DDT in its body fat than the tiny animals did, but not enough to hurt it.

Each big fish eats lots of little fish. The bigger fish has more DDT in its body fat, but not enough to hurt it.

Each heron eats lots of big fish. The level of DDT is high enough now to poison the heron.

> When people realised the terrible effect of DDT, it was banned in this country and many others. Now DDT is only used in countries where the pests do so much damage that it is worth using DDT.

Heroes and villains

Pesticides are very important. Without them, at least half of the food grown in the world would be eaten by pests. Many people in the world are starving today, but without pesticides there would be millions and millions more.

But pesticides can be killers. They are all poisonous chemicals, and like DDT they can build up in a food chain. Before any chemical is used, it must be tested very carefully to make sure that no animals, including people, will be poisoned along the food chain.

What do you know?

1 Here are some of the ways people get involved in food webs. For each one, decide whether its main effect on the environment will be good or bad. Explain why.

- emptying sewage in the sea
- planting marram grass on sand dunes
- putting waste from factories into rivers
- making nature reserves
- stopping whale hunting
- spraying crops with pesticides

2 DDT is still used in some places in the world. In Africa, the disease called malaria kills lots of people. DDT is used to destroy the mosquitoes that spread malaria. What do you think are the good and the bad things about this?

Key ideas

When people **manage** a habitat, they control what happens to the plants and animals there.

People can have a good or bad effect when they interfere in food webs.

Some pesticides like DDT build up in a food chain. They poison the animals at the top of the pyramid.

Adaptation

4f How many fleas on a hedgehog?

Most of us think hedgehogs are rather appealing animals. But what most of us don't know is that hedgehogs are the habitat of the hedgehog flea!

a How many fleas do you think a single hedgehog will support?

A flea-ometer?

The fleas on a hedgehog are called a **population**. This is a group of animals or plants of the same species living in the same habitat. We study a species by finding out how many organisms are in a population. Their numbers tell us something about the conditions they live in. A healthy hedgehog will carry a lot of fleas!

The numbers game

The numbers of animals or plants in a population will vary as a result of all sorts of changes in their physical surroundings (their **environment**).

Temperature has a big effect on populations. Most animals and plants grow faster when it is warmer. Tadpoles turn into frogs early in the year. This means they have plenty of time as adult frogs to feed and grow before winter arrives. More of them will survive, and the frog population will go up.

Light also affects the numbers of organisms, particularly plants. If there is less sunlight than usual, plants grow more slowly and they are less likely to flower. If they don't flower they don't produce seeds, which reduces the size of the population next year.

b 1 What do you think caused the loss of the tree population in this photograph?

2 What other populations might have been affected at the same time?

Sometimes unusual weather conditions can affect the populations of plants and animals.

58

The amount of water can make a huge difference to the numbers of animals and plants in a habitat. A mass of flowers grow in the desert after a rare downfall of rain. The water allows thousands of seeds to germinate. They grow into plants, flower and make more seeds. The plants also feed many animals, so their populations can increase too.

The ups and downs of life

As you can see from this graph, the numbers in a population don't stay the same every year. More great tits survive in some years than in others.

c 1 In which year do you think conditions were particularly good for the great tits?

2 In which year do you think they were really bad?

It is not only the physical conditions of the environment that affect the populations of living things. The activities of other animals and plants, and of people too, can have a big effect on populations.

2 Look at the graph showing the changes in the population of great tits. What sort of things do you think would affect the numbers of small birds like these?

3 Here are two different populations. For each one describe what might make the population go up and what might make it go down.
a head lice on a small child
b weeds in a garden

What do you know?

1 Copy and complete the following sentences. Use the words below to fill the gaps.

> bad   environment   temperature
> population   weather   up

The number of animals or plants in a _____ goes up and down, depending on the conditions in the _____. If conditions are _____ the numbers in a population go down, but when things go well the numbers go _____. Populations are affected by _____, light and _____.

Key ideas

A **population** is a group of organisms of the same species living in the same habitat.

The number of organisms in a population will change as a result of things such as temperature, light and weather conditions.

Adaptation

4g A question of balance

A woodland looks a peaceful place. But if we look at the food web it supports we see a very different picture!

a Name animals that eat:

1 seeds made by the trees (acorns, nuts and cones)

2 worms   3 beetles   4 mice.

Animal competitions

In a food web there is always **competition**. Different species of animals compete with each other for food. The winners of the competition get the most food, so they are most likely to survive. They are likely to have large populations.

In any habitat there will be several species of **herbivores** (plant eaters). They can live side by side because they eat slightly different diets. But when food is in short supply, they are in competition because they are all trying to eat the same plants.

Carnivores (meat eaters) also compete with each other for food. Each species eats a different combination of other animals, so they usually all survive. When times are hard because there are fewer animals to eat, the competition hots up and the losers die.

Plant competitions

Plants make their own food by photosynthesis using sunlight. Plants don't compete for food, but they compete for light. The tallest trees spread their leaves to catch as much light as possible. This means there is less light underneath them for the shorter plants. These grow in any patch of light left, all struggling to be the tallest.

Plants compete for water and minerals from the soil as well. They have different shaped roots to get what they need from the soil. Some roots go deep, others are spread out.

Family feuds

Different species compete with each other. But animals and plants of the same species compete with each other as well. Male blackbirds fight in a garden to get the best nesting place. Pet cats fight over a bowl of food. When there is plenty of food, every member of a species gets enough. But when food is scarce, only the winners of the competition (the fittest) survive.

Getting in first

The competition between different species can be very fierce. Giant tortoises survived on the Galapagos Islands for thousands of years. Then sailors let free some goats on one of the islands. The goat population grew so fast and ate so much that the tortoises could not compete. In 1960 the last tortoise on the island died.

What do you know?

1 Copy and complete the following sentences. Use the words below to fill the gaps.

plenty	water	fittest	compete	food
	scarce	light		

Animals and plants _____ with each other for the things they need. Animals compete with each other to get the most _____. Plants compete for _____, _____ and minerals. When there is _____ of food everyone survives, but when food is _____ only the _____ survive.

2a Think of two examples of plants or animals of the same species competing with each other.
b Think of two examples of different species of animals or plants competing with each other.

Key ideas

Two or more living things can **compete** against each other for things they need like food, water and light.

Competition affects the size of a population.

Adaptation

4h Babies mean success

When there are plenty of plants growing, there is plenty of food for the herbivores. They all do well and have lots of offspring. This means there is plenty of food for the carnivores and they also do well. This keeps everything in balance. Without the carnivores, there would be so many herbivores they would run out of plants to eat.

More of the best

There are two ways to increase your population:

- You can have more offspring.
- You can make sure that all your offspring survive to go on and have offspring themselves.

In any ecosystem, some organisms do better than others. The animals or plants that are well suited to their habitat will compete successfully for food or light. This means that they will reproduce more successfully. More of their offspring will survive. The animals and plants that do best will become the **dominant species**.

Successful species

One dandelion in a lawn this summer probably means there will be lots of them next year. Dandelions are very tough and compete well. They produce many seeds which are spread far and wide, so we see lots of dandelions.

Rabbits are pests to farmers. They nibble grass very closely, and they also reproduce very rapidly. A well fed female rabbit can have several litters each year. The offspring quickly start having more babies themselves.

A successful rabbit population can strip fields of the grass grown for sheep and cattle. Foxes get rid of only a small number of these rabbits. The biggest predator of rabbits is humans.

Caring for the babies

Some organisms produce very large numbers of offspring and leave them to compete on their own. Plants, many fish and insects do this. Because there are so many offspring, some of them will probably survive.

Other organisms produce fewer offspring, but they try and make sure that their offspring survive. Most of the larger mammals and some birds do this.

Rabbits do both. They produce quite a few offspring and look after them both before and after birth.

a Think of some of the most successful organisms you know. How do they make sure that their offspring survive better than everyone else's?

What do you know?

1 Answer these questions, using complete sentences.
a What are the two ways of increasing a population?
b What do we call the animals and plants that do best in an ecosystem?
c Name three species that produce lots of offspring but do not care for them.
d Name three species that produce small numbers of offspring, but take care of them to try and make sure they survive.

2a Why are rabbits such successful animals?
b What is the effect of the success of rabbits on **i** foxes **ii** farmers?

3 There is often competition between people and other species.
a Give an example of people competing with other living organisms.
b In this sort of competition, people usually win. Why is this?

Key ideas

The most successful organisms are good at reproducing. More of their offspring survive to have offspring themselves.

Adaptation 4 EXTRAS

4b A rocky home

Some habitats are a real challenge to the organisms that live in them. On a rocky shore there will be lots of rock pools like this one, which form little habitats called **microhabitats**. Depending on their position on the beach, they spend from a few minutes to several hours every day out of the water. The rest of the time they are under the sea. The organisms that live in them or are trapped in them have some problems!

Look at the animals and plants shown in this rock pool. When the rocks are covered by the sea, they have a cool environment which changes very little.

1 Make a list of the possible difficulties in the habitat once the rock pool is uncovered when the tide goes out.

2 How do you think the organisms in a rock pool cope with the problems they have to face?

4d Pyramids of biomass

The numbers of organisms in a food chain can produce very oddly shaped pyramids. Instead of counting organisms, we can measure the amount of biological material or biomass at each level of a food chain. This always gives us a sensibly shaped pyramid. There is always more plant material than animal material. Biomass is used at each level of the chain, so there is less biomass towards the top of the pyramid.

1 Sketch a pyramid of biomass for the following food chains:
a grass ⟶ rabbit ⟶ fox
b rose bush ⟶ greenfly ⟶ ladybird
c grass ⟶ zebra ⟶ lion

The problem is that biomass is not very easy to measure. Biomass is all the biological material in an organism **without** the water.

2 Why can't we measure the biomass of living things?

3 It is easier to measure the biomass of plants than of animals. Why is this?

4e Improving on nature?

People often change the natural environment to meet their own needs. This is called managing the environment. We grow different crops each year so that different minerals are taken from the soil. We build drainage ditches to prevent flooding. We make pathways and plant new trees so we can enjoy the countryside.

1 Choose an environment you know. It could be part of your school grounds, a garden or a park, or a local river bank or woodland. Describe it carefully, with sketches to help. Make a plan to show how you would manage the environment. Include simple ways of making it easier for people to use and better for the organisms living there.

4g The spread of populations

Some populations of animals and plants have a very high **density**. This means that the organisms live very close to each other. The grass in the lawn, the ants in an ants' nest and zebra in a herd are all examples of this. Other populations have a very low density. The individuals in the population are scattered far apart through the habitat. Polar bears are an example.

The three most common patterns found in populations are shown in the diagram.

Clumped species are most common. Herds or groups of animals and plants clump together near the resources they need.

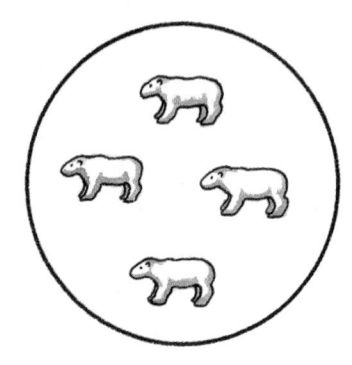

Evenly spread populations are common in large carnivores.

Individuals are **randomly spread** when there are plenty of resources and no fierce competition.

1a Give three examples of populations which occur in clumps.
b Living in a herd near the resources you need is a good reason for clumping together. Can you think of another advantage to animals of living in a herd?

2a Give three examples of animals which live alone most of the time and are evenly spread out.
b Why do you think this is most common amongst large carnivores?

3 In a wood full of bluebells, some areas have many more plants than others. Why do you think this might be?

Solar system

5a Once a day

Each day, the Sun rises in the east, moves across the sky and sets in the west.

If you have a compass, you can use it to help you stand facing due south. Then the Sun rises on your left and sets on your right.

a In which direction is the Sun at midday?

Night and day

For a long time, people thought that the Sun went round the Earth. They thought it took just one day for the Sun to make a complete journey around the Earth. This was not a silly idea, because that is what appears to happen. However, nowadays we know that it is a wrong idea.

Now we know that the Earth is shaped like a sphere, and it spins around. This is what makes the Sun seem to move around the Earth. It takes just 24 hours for the Earth to make one complete turn.

It is daytime on the side of the Earth facing the Sun. It is night-time on the other side.

The Earth spins from west to east, so that the Sun appears to move from east to west.

b Make a rough copy of this picture of the Earth, and draw an arrow to show which way it turns.

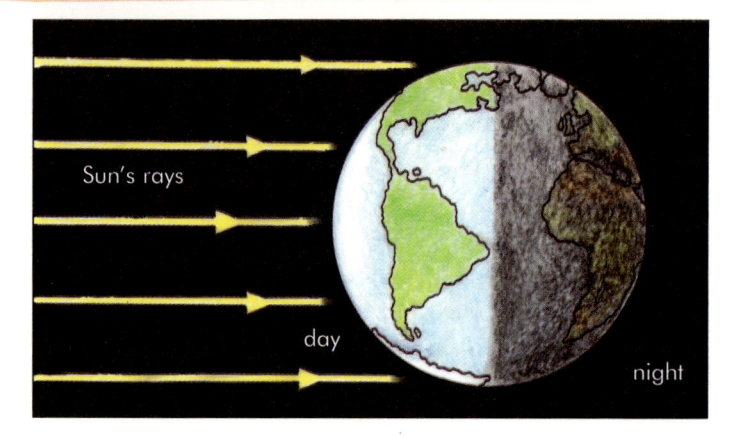

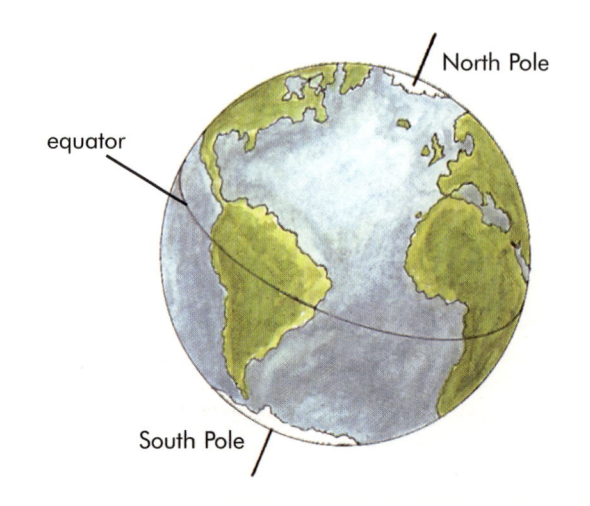

66

Points of view

In the UK we are in the northern hemisphere, the half of the Earth north of the equator. We are quite a long way north of the equator. If you were in South Africa, which is quite a long way south of the equator, things would be different. You would have to look north to see where the Sun was in the sky.

c 1 Would the Sun rise on your left or on your right? On which side of you would it set?

2 Would the Sun rise in the east or in the west?

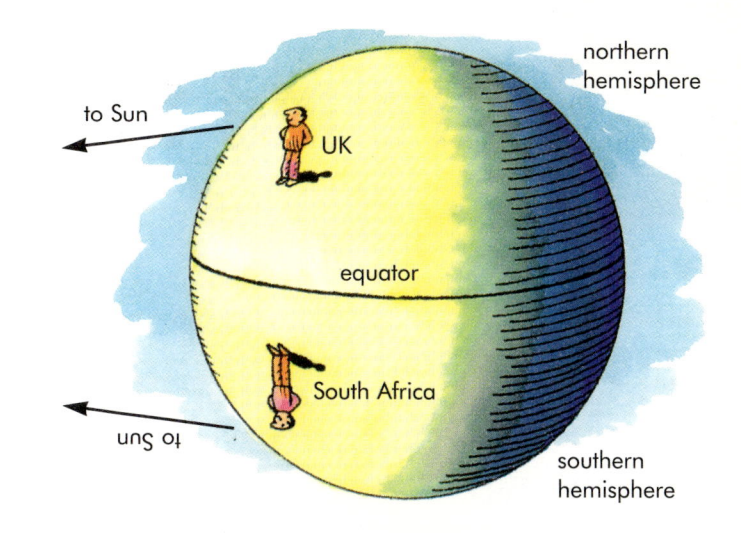

Night watch

If it's a clear night, you can see the stars. If you watch carefully, you will see that they move across the sky in just the same way that the Sun does. They rise in the east and set in the west.

The photograph shows a picture of the stars. The camera's shutter was left open for an hour. The stars moved across the sky, making bright tracks across the photograph.

d Explain why stars appear to move across the sky from east to west.

What do you know?

1 Sophie's window faces south. She has drawn the view from her window, and marked where the Sun is at dawn. Sketch the picture and mark where the Sun will be at midday, and at dusk (when it is setting).

2 People have been to the Moon. From the Moon's surface, you can look at the Earth. Explain what you would expect to see if you watched the Earth for 24 hours.

Key ideas

The Sun and the other stars seem to move round the Earth from east to west. In fact, it is the Earth that is turning round the other way.

It takes 24 hours for one complete turn.

67

Solar system

5b Around the Sun

The Earth is just one of the planets in the **solar system**. The Sun is at the centre of the solar system. All of the planets go round the Sun. The path of a planet around the Sun is called its **orbit**. The picture shows the planets and their orbits.

a 1 Which planet is closest to the Sun?
   2 Which planet is furthest from the Sun?

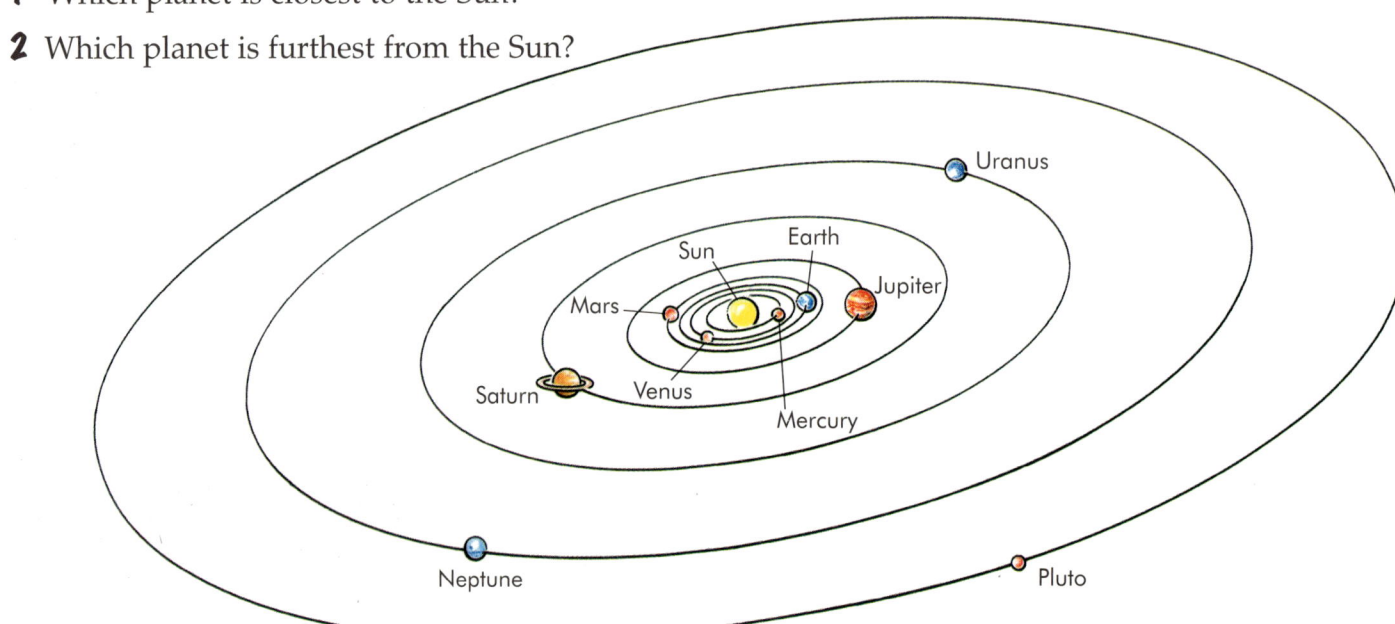

A problem of scale

The Earth is very small compared with the Sun, and it is tiny compared with the whole of the solar system.

In this model, the Sun is a large ball, 50 cm in diameter. The Earth is a small bead, just 5 mm across. The Earth is 100 m from the Sun. The table on the opposite page shows the models for the planets.

68

b Why do you think Uranus, Neptune and Pluto are missing from the model?

Planet	Model of planet	Diameter	Distance from Sun
Mercury	pin head	1.5 mm	40 m
Venus	bead	5 mm	75 m
Earth	bead	5 mm	100 m
Mars	bead	2.5 mm	160 m
Jupiter	tennis ball	6 cm	540 m
Saturn	tennis ball	5 cm	1000 m

Gravity's pull

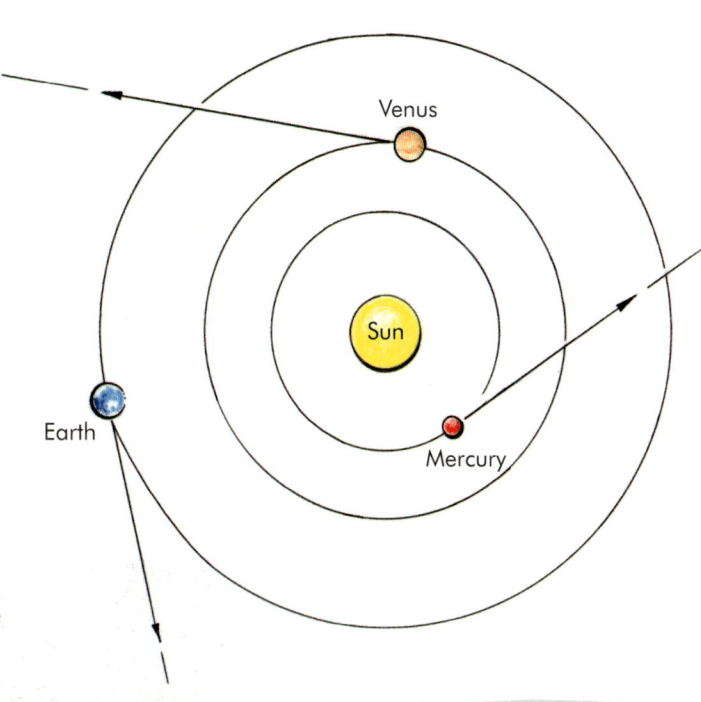

The pull of the Sun's **gravity** keeps the Earth in its orbit around the Sun. The Sun's pull is like the pull of the string on a conker, as you whirl it around your head. If you let go, then there is no force pulling inwards on the conker. It flies off, away from you.

If the Sun's gravity ever stopped pulling, the Earth and all the other planets would fly off into space.

The Sun is a very large object, and so the pull of its gravity is very strong. Its gravity will never stop working, so long as the Sun still exists.

What do you know?

1 Copy and complete the following sentences. Choose the correct word from each pair.

In the solar system, the **stars/planets** travel round the **Sun/Moon**. They are held in their orbits by the **push/pull** of the Sun's **gravity/string**.

2 The Moon travels round the Earth. It follows a circular path. What force do you think keeps the Moon going round the Earth?

3 Look at the table above. It shows information about six of the planets. Make a list of them in order of size, starting with the biggest and ending with the smallest.

Key ideas

The Sun is at the centre of the **solar system**. The planets travel round the Sun in their **orbits**.

The pull of the Sun's **gravity** keeps the planets in their orbits. Without gravity, the planets would fly off into space.

Solar system

5c All in a year

It takes the Earth just one year to travel all the way round its orbit around the Sun. Each planet travels at a different speed around its orbit, and takes a different length of time to make a complete orbit.

Mercury travels faster than any other planet, and it has the shortest distance to travel. It takes only 3 months to travel round the Sun, the shortest time of all the planets.

a How many times does Mercury travel round its orbit in one year?

Planet	Time for one orbit
Mercury	3 months
Venus	7 months
Earth	12 months
Mars	23 months
Jupiter	142 months
Saturn	354 months
Uranus	1008 months
Neptune	1978 months
Pluto	2976 months

Seeing stars

At night, we can see the pattern of the stars in the sky. As the Earth travels round the Sun, the pattern changes. From the picture, you can see why this is.

In June, we look out and see the stars in one direction. In December, the Earth has travelled round to the other side of the Sun. We are facing in the opposite direction, so we see the stars that lie in the other direction.

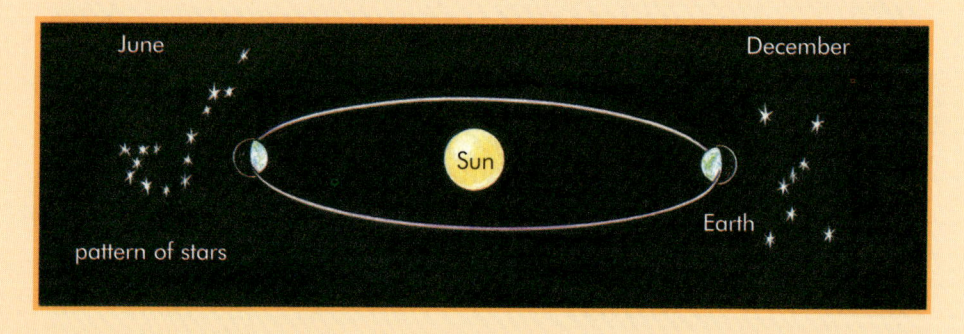

The seasons

In northern Europe we have four seasons, spring, summer, autumn and winter. In the summer, the Sun moves high up in the sky. In the winter, it is much lower in the sky.

70

The tilted Earth

The Earth spins around its **axis**. The axis passes through the Earth from the North Pole to the South Pole. The Earth spinning around its axis gives us night and day.

The Earth moving around its orbit gives us the seasons. The Earth's axis is **tilted**. In June, the northern hemisphere is tilted towards the Sun. We see the Sun high in the sky, and this gives us our hot summers.

In December, the northern hemisphere is tilted away from the Sun. We see the Sun low in the sky, and this gives us our cold winters.

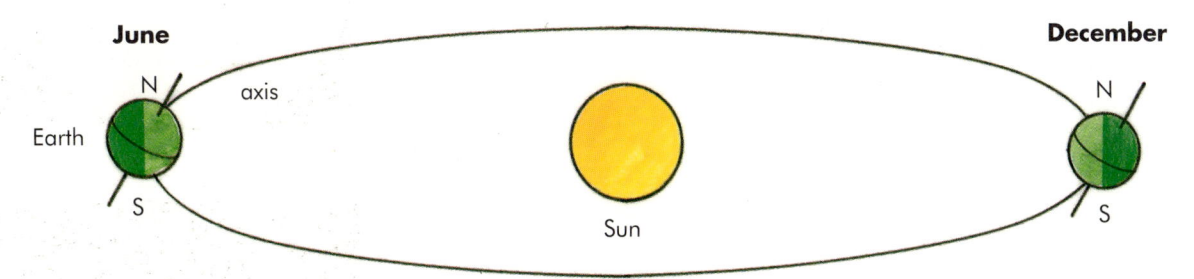

b Which way is the southern hemisphere tilted in June? What season is this?

What do you know?

1 The answers to all of these questions are numbers.
a How many months does it take for the Earth to travel once around its orbit?
b How many hours does it take for the Earth to spin once around its axis?
c How many seasons do we experience in one year, in northern Europe?

2 The sentences below were written by an Australian pupil to explain the seasons. Copy and complete the sentences. Choose the correct word from each pair.

In June, the southern hemisphere is tilted **towards/away from** the Sun. We see the Sun **high/low** in the sky, and this gives us our **hot/cold summers/winters**.

3 If the Earth's axis was not tilted, we would not have seasons. Each day would be the same. The Sun would always rise at 6 a.m. and set at 6 p.m. The temperature would be like an average day in March or September. What would you miss if we had no summer or winter?

Key ideas

The Earth takes one complete year to travel round its orbit around the Sun. We see different stars in the winter sky than in the summer sky because the Earth is pointing the other way.

The Sun moves higher in the sky during the summer than during the winter. This is because the Earth's **axis** is **tilted**. The tilt makes the northern hemisphere face towards the Sun in the summer, and away from the Sun in the winter. This is why we have seasons.

Solar system

5d Hot stars, cold planets

Our Sun is a star. It is a source of heat and light. You can feel its heat energy on your skin and see its light with your eyes. There are many more stars like our Sun, a long way off in space.

Seeing stars

You can see thousands of stars if you look at the night sky using binoculars. You may have noticed that different stars have different colours. Their colour depends on how hot they are.

Colour	Appearance	Temperature
red		3000 °C
orange		4000 °C
yellow		6000 °C
white		10 000 °C
blue-white		20 000 °C

a 1 A red giant star is an enormous star, much bigger than the Sun. It looks red. What is the temperature of a red giant?

2 The surface of the Sun looks yellow. What is its temperature?

⚠ **Warning**
Never look directly at the Sun as you could permanently damage your eyesight.

Visiting the planets

It would be impossible to visit the Sun. Your spacecraft would evaporate when it came near to the hot surface.

It would be possible to visit one of the other planets in the solar system. Planets are not as hot as the Sun. The planets are warmed by the Sun's rays, and we can see them because they reflect some of the rays back into space. We see the Moon because it reflects the Sun's light.

The evening star

Venus is sometimes called the 'evening star', although it is not a star but a planet. You can often see it, shining brightly, low in the west, in the evening sky. It is reflecting light from the Sun into our eyes.

If you look at Venus through a telescope, you may see that only part of it is lit up. On one side of Venus it is daytime, and on the other side it is night-time. The daytime side is reflecting the Sun's rays. The Sun's rays do not reach the other side.

Venus is the brightest star.

Venus seen through a telescope

▶ **b** Copy this picture of Venus. Label the two sides **day** and **night**. Show how rays of light from the Sun are reflected off the planet.

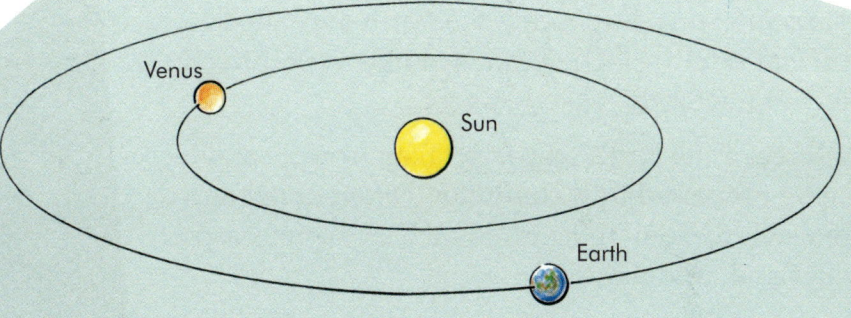

What do you know?

1 Copy and complete the following table. Use the words below to fill the boxes.

Sun planets stars Moon	
sources of light	
seen by reflected light	

2 Pluto is a long way from the Sun. It is very cold on Pluto. Its temperature is −230 °C! Write the things in this list in order, from coldest to hottest.

Earth   red giant star   Pluto   Sun
white dwarf star

3 Copy the diagram above which shows the Sun, the Earth and Venus. Draw a ray of light from the Sun. Show how it is reflected by Venus and reaches the Earth, so that we are able to see Venus.

Key ideas

The Sun is very hot. We can see the Sun and the other stars because they are sources of their own light.

The planets are colder than the Sun. We can see the other planets from the Earth because they reflect the Sun's light.

Solar system

5e Exploring space

When the first people went to the Moon, they could look back at the Earth. One astronaut said he felt that the whole of the Earth was 'home'.

From space, you can see the blue sea and the white clouds.

a What other features can you see in this picture of the Earth?

A different view

Spacecraft travelling round the Earth are called artificial **satellites**. They can give us a very different view of the Earth.

Pictures of the Earth's surface taken from a satellite can be processed by a computer. Different colours are used to show up features such as towns, crops, water and mountains.

b What colours are towns, water and high mountains on this photograph?

This table shows some uses of artificial satellites.

weather forecasting	satellites can see clouds and detect atmospheric pressure
spying	satellites can see military bases and troop movements
space exploration	satellites can travel to other planets and to the Moon
communications	satellites can broadcast television programmes and transmit telephone calls around the Earth
Earth observation	satellites can detect crops, forests, rocks and other features
navigation	satellites can send signals to help ships and aircraft find their way around the Earth

c Discuss some of these uses of artificial satellites. How can they help to do these different things?

74

Long distance information

The other planets are a long way from the Earth. We can't see them clearly from Earth because the view is spoilt by the Earth's atmosphere.

Many spacecraft have now travelled out into the solar system, to have a closer look at the planets. Some have even landed on the surfaces of Mars and Venus, and they have sent back pictures to show us what these planets are like.

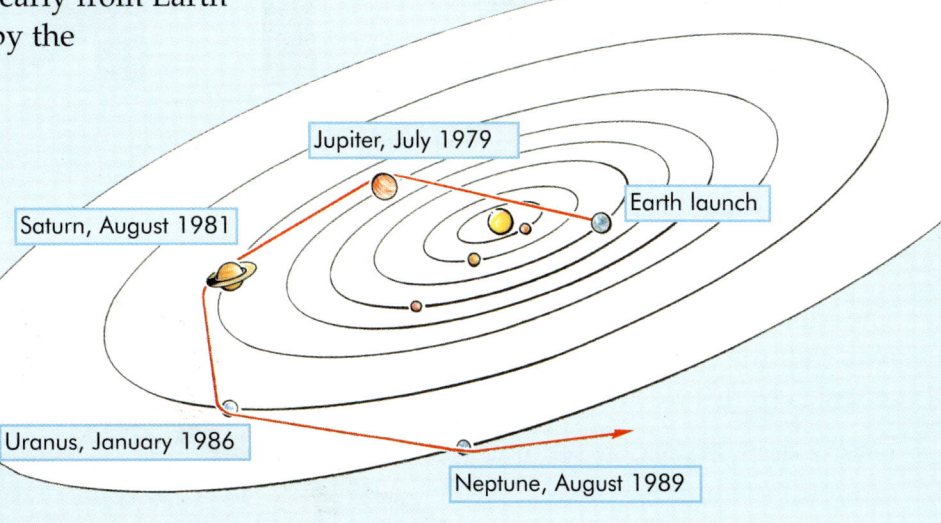

Jupiter, July 1979
Saturn, August 1981
Earth launch
Uranus, January 1986
Neptune, August 1989

Voyager 2 was launched in 1977. It has travelled past several planets and sent photographs back to Earth. It is now travelling out past the orbit of Pluto, beyond the edge of the solar system.

d Make a list of the planets Voyager 2 visited on its journey through space.

What do you know?

1 Copy and complete the following sentences. Use the words below to fill the gaps.

| planets | Earth | space | satellites |

Artificial _____ travel through _____. They send back useful information about the _____ and other _____.

2 Satellites like Voyager 2 are called 'artificial', because they are made by people. The Earth has one satellite that travels around it which is not artificial. What is it?

3 The spacecraft that visited Mars and Venus found no signs of life. What would you look for if you were exploring another planet and you wanted to know if there was any life there? What do all living things need?

Key ideas

It is difficult to see the other planets from the Earth because they are so far away, and because the Earth's atmosphere gets in the way. Spacecraft have visited most of the planets, so we know a lot more about them than we used to.

Satellites are useful for finding out more about the Earth.

Solar system

5 EXTRAS

5a The moving Moon

The Moon moves across the sky in the same way that the Sun does. It rises in the east and sets in the west.

1 Why does the Moon seem to move around the Earth like this?

If you watch the Moon for several days, you will see that its position changes from day to day. The picture shows the position of the Moon at 9 o'clock on different evenings. It moves slowly across the sky.

2 These observations show that the Moon goes round the Earth. Which way round does it go?

5b Life without gravity

The pull of gravity keeps us on the ground. It keeps the Moon in its orbit around the Earth, and the planets in their orbits around the Sun. Gravity holds the Sun together.

1 Imagine that gravity gradually got weaker and weaker. What effects would we observe?

5c A different Earth

Standing on the surface of the Earth, it is hard to imagine that the Earth is a giant sphere, spinning around and moving round its orbit. We can't feel any of this movement. Can you imagine what it would be like to live on a different Earth?

1 Suppose that we lived on an Earth whose axis was not tilted. What would we notice?

2 The Earth's orbit around the Sun is almost circular. Suppose we lived on an Earth whose orbit was shaped like an ellipse (a squashed circle). What would we notice?

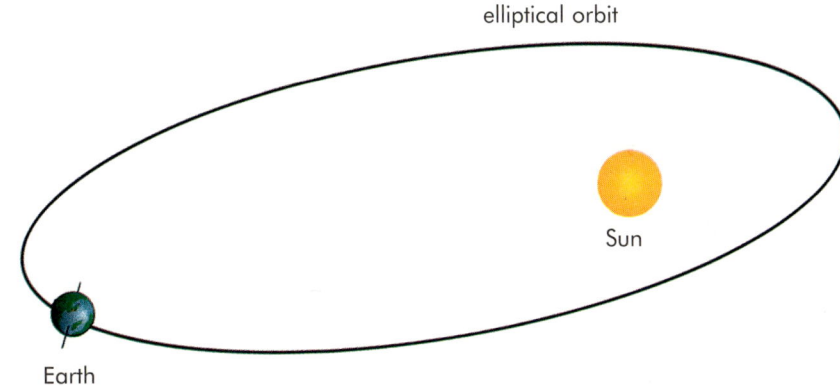

5e Voyager's voyage

Look at the picture on page 75 which shows the path followed by Voyager 2 as it explored the solar system. Voyager did not always travel in a straight line.

1 Explain why Voyager had to change direction each time it passed a planet.

2 The planets provided a pull to make Voyager change direction. What force gave this pull?

3 What can you say about the forces on Voyager when it was close to a big planet, such as Jupiter?

4 What can you say about the forces on Voyager when it was far from any of the planets?

Acids and alkalis

6a Suck a lemon!

Do you pull a face like this when you taste a lemon? Lemons have a sharp, sour taste. Unripe fruits have the same kind of sourness, so you know not to eat them.

The chemicals that give this sour taste are called **acids**. In small amounts, acids can be quite refreshing, like the citric acid in lemon drinks. But many acids are poisonous.

Dangerous acids

Some acids are very **corrosive**. They eat away at materials such as metal, or clothing, or even you!

Car batteries contain sulphuric acid. This acid will dissolve iron, so the battery case is made of a special plastic that is not attacked by acid. You have to be very careful if you move a car battery. If you drop it, the case will break, spilling this dangerous acid.

Using acids

In some areas, layers of hard white limescale form in kettles and around taps. Acids can be used to dissolve this limescale away. The limescale fizzes as it dissolves in the acid.

a Is this a physical or chemical change?

Kettle cleaners use fairly **weak acids** such as citric acid. This is strong enough to remove the limescale, but will not harm a metal kettle. Some toilet cleaners use **strong acids** such as hydrochloric acid. The porcelain toilet bowl is resistant to the acid, so it is not harmed. You have to be very careful not to spill any acid.

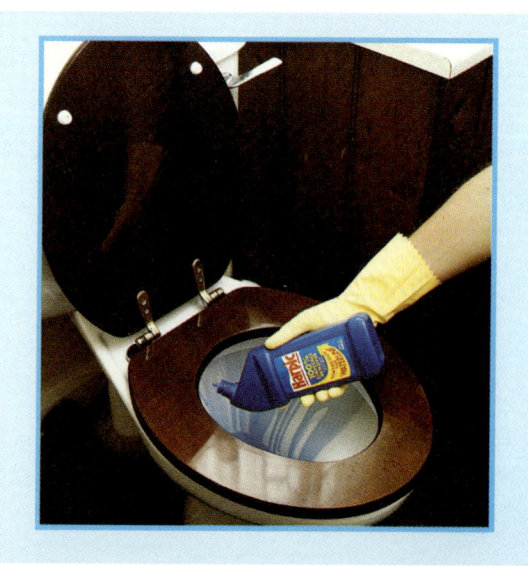

The opposite of an acid

There is another family of chemicals that are often used for cleaning. Soap is used to remove dirt from your skin. Detergents are used to remove grease and dirt from clothes and to do the washing-up. Washing soda is used in some kitchen and bathroom cleaners.

These chemicals are called **alkalis**. In many ways they are the opposite of acids. However, like acids, strong alkalis are very corrosive. Sodium hydroxide eats into grease and is often used to clean ovens.

b Make a list of the alkalis you might find at home. What are they used for?

c Why must you wear rubber gloves if you are cleaning an oven?

Just add water

Acids and alkalis only show their properties when they are dissolved in water. If you sprinkle dry citric acid crystals onto limescale, nothing happens. It only starts to fizz if you add water.

Alkalis must also dissolve in water before they can react.

What do you know?

1 Copy and complete the following sentences. Use the words below to fill the gaps.

| corrosive | sour | alkali | sulphuric | citric acid |

Lemon juice contains a chemical called _____ _____. This has a _____ taste. Stronger acids such as _____ acid are very _____ and will dissolve some metals.

Washing soda is an _____. This is the opposite of an acid.

2 Give two different uses for citric acid at home.

3 Vinegar has a sour taste. Is it an acid or an alkali?

4 What do strong acids and strong alkalis have in common?

5 Why is washing soda dissolved in water before it is used to clean floors?

Key ideas

Some natural chemicals have a sour taste. They are called **acids**. Strong acids are **corrosive**.

Alkalis are the opposite of acids. Strong alkalis are also corrosive.

Acids and alkalis show their properties when they are dissolved in water.

Acids and alkalis

6b Telling them apart

How can you tell acids and alkalis apart? You can't taste them to see if they are sour, because some are poisonous and others would burn you. They can both be corrosive.

The cabbage test

Do you like red cabbage? If you eat it raw, it's a purple-red colour. If you like it pickled, it's a much brighter red.

Vinegar is used to pickle cabbage, and vinegar is a solution of acetic acid in water. The acid makes the cabbage turn bright red. If you put red cabbage into an alkaline solution, however, it turns blue!

The dye in the cabbage tells you whether it is in an acid or an alkali. Dyes like this are called **indicators.**

The litmus test

Litmus is another indicator dye. Litmus turns red when it is in an acid and blue when it is in an alkali, just like red cabbage. To test a liquid, you dip litmus paper in it.

- An acid will turn blue litmus paper red.
- An alkali will turn red litmus paper blue.

All change!

Not all indicators are red in acids and blue in alkalis. Have you ever used colour-change felt-tipped pens? The ink changes colour when you go over it with the 'magic' pen. The 'magic' pen contains an alkali, and the inks are indicators.

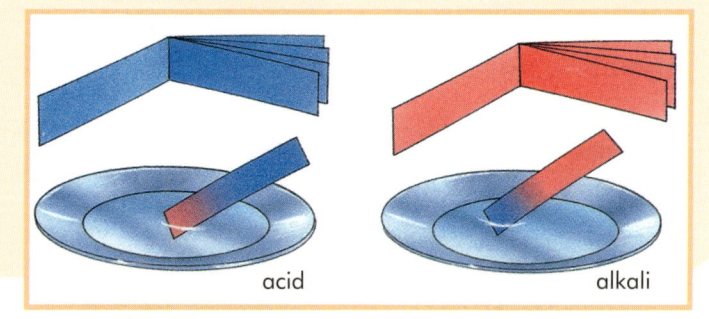

The pH scale

Litmus just tells you whether something is acidic or alkaline. **Universal indicator** is another sort of indicator. It is made from a special mixture of dyes. It turns different colours in different strengths of acid or alkali.

The different strengths of acid or alkali are measured on the **pH scale**. The strongest acid is number 1 on this scale and the strongest alkali is number 14. You can use universal indicator to find the pH number for any liquid.

The picture shows two universal indicator colour charts. Exactly in the middle of the pH scale, at number 7, is water. Pure water is neither acidic nor alkaline. It is **neutral**.

a Vijay used universal indicator solution to test some liquids. Make a table with column heads **Substance**, **pH**, **Acid or alkali**, **Strength**. Fill it in using the results below.

1 Crushed nettle stings
2 A kitchen cleaner
3 Sugar solution
4 Baking soda
5 Battery acid
6 Cola

pH	Universal indicator solution		
1		hydrochloric acid	**strongest acid**
2		lemon juice	
3		orange juice	
4		vinegar	
5		black coffee	**weak acids**
6		rainwater	
7		pure water	**neutral**
8		sea water baking soda	
9		milk of magnesia	**weak alkalis**
10		soap	
11			
12		washing soda	
13			
14		oven cleaner sodium hydroxide	**strongest alkali**

Universal indicator is also used in pH papers, which give different colours.

pH 1 2 3 4 5 6 7 8 9 10 11 12 13 14

What do you know?

1 Copy and complete the following sentences. Use the words below to fill the gaps.

| pH | litmus | indicators | 7 | universal |

_____ change colour in acids or alkalis. _____ is an indicator which turns red in acids and blue in alkalis. _____ indicator changes colour with the _____ scale. Neutral water has a pH of _____ .

2 What colour would litmus turn in:
a lemon juice
b washing soda solution
c soap solution
d vinegar?

3 Wet cement harms your skin.
a How could you tell if cement is an acid or an alkali?
b Is it a weak or strong acid or alkali?

Key ideas

Indicators change colour with acids and alkalis.

Acids turn blue litmus red. Alkalis turn red litmus blue.

The **pH scale** is used to measure the strength of acids and alkalis. Low numbers are strong acids. High numbers are strong alkalis.

Water is **neutral**, at pH7.

Acids and alkalis

6c Cancelling out

If you could put universal indicator paper inside your stomach, it would turn red! Your stomach contains strong hydrochloric acid. This helps to digest your food. Your stomach has a special lining to protect it from this corrosive acid.

The acid can sometimes bubble up out of your stomach. It gives you a burning feeling. This is called **acid indigestion**.

a How do you cure acid indigestion?

Antacids to the rescue!

At the chemist's, you can buy different types of **antacids**. These help get rid of some of the acid in your stomach. 'Antacid' means 'anti-acid', the opposite of an acid.

b Can you guess what is in an antacid?

One antacid is milk of magnesia. Universal indicator paper shows that milk of magnesia is an alkali.

When you mix an acid with an alkali, they cancel out. They leave a neutral liquid behind. This is called **neutralisation**.

$$\text{acid} + \text{alkali} \xrightarrow{\text{neutralisation}} \text{neutral solution}$$

Alkalis and bases

Milk of magnesia is magnesium hydroxide in water. Some of the magnesium hydroxide dissolves in the water, and gives an alkaline solution. But some antacids come as tablets which do not dissolve in water. The chemicals are insoluble. They cannot affect pH paper, so they are not alkalis, but they can still neutralise acids. They are **bases**.

All substances that neutralise acids are bases.

Alkalis are bases that dissolve in water.

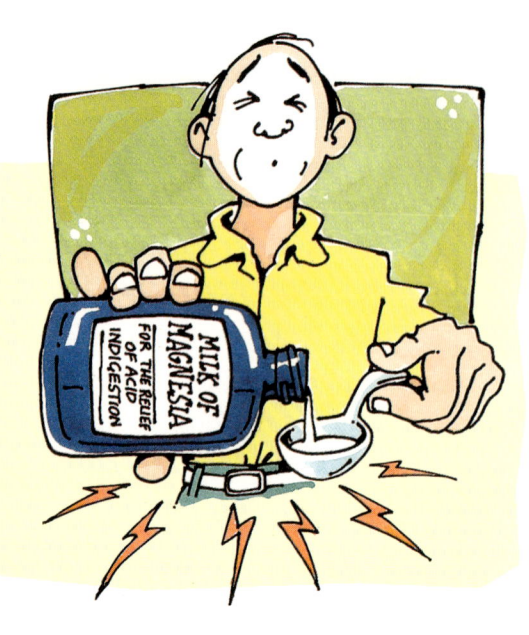

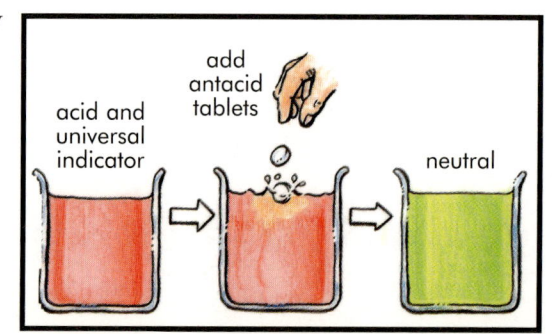

$$\text{acid} + \text{base} \xrightarrow{\text{neutralisation}} \text{neutral solution}$$

The trouble with soil

Most plants grow best if the soil is neutral or slightly acidic (pH6–7). But in some places, the soil is very acidic. The peat soils on the moors of Yorkshire and Scotland may have a pH as low as 3 or 4. This is fine for pine forests, but is no good for crops.

Soils like this need an antacid too! For hundreds of years, farmers have improved the soil by sprinkling it with lime. This neutralises the excess acid in the soil.

Be a soil detective

Farmer Giles is having trouble with his crops. He's sent you a bag of soil to test.

c Describe how you could find the pH of the soil.

d If universal indicator showed pH4, what would you advise Farmer Giles to do?

What do you know?

1a Why does your stomach have to have a special lining?
b What causes acid indigestion?
c What happens if you take milk of magnesia?

2 If you use universal indicator in solution:
a What colour would it be in lemon juice?
b Describe what would happen to it if you kept adding a solution of washing soda to lemon juice until all the acid was gone.
c How would you know that there was no acid left?
d What would happen if you then added extra washing soda solution?

3 Explain the following sentence. 'All alkalis are bases, but not all bases are alkalis.'

Key ideas

Acids and **bases** cancel each other out. This is called **neutralisation**.

Alkalis are bases that dissolve in water.

Acids and alkalis

6d Making salts

What happens during neutralisation? Dilute hydrochloric acid is a colourless liquid. Dilute sodium hydroxide solution is a colourless liquid. If you mix them together you get ... a colourless liquid!

If you test this liquid with universal indicator paper, you will find that it is neutral. But if you let the water evaporate away, you will see crystals start to grow. A new substance has formed during neutralisation. It is something you are very familiar with. It is common salt, the stuff you sprinkle on your chips!

Where did the salt come from?

An acid and a base react to form a new chemical called a **salt**. Water is also formed during this reaction. You can write this as a word equation:

acid + base ⟶ salt + water

You can make different salts by using different acids and bases. The pictures show some of these salts.

Potassium chloride is used in medicine for diarrhoea.

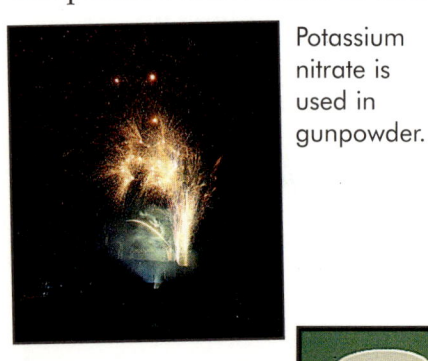

Potassium nitrate is used in gunpowder.

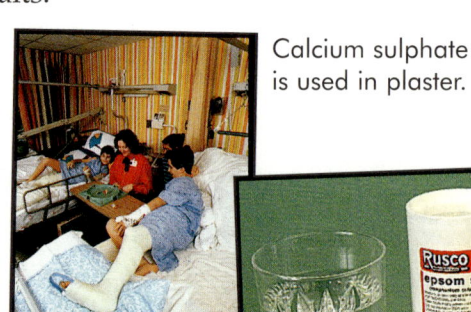

Calcium sulphate is used in plaster.

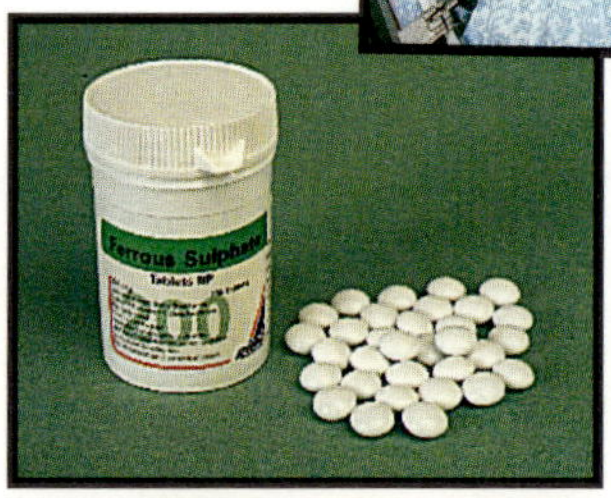

Iron sulphate is used in iron tablets. People take these to help their blood carry oxygen.

Magnesium sulphate is used in medicine for constipation.

Copper chloride is used to cure fish fungus.

How to name a salt

The names of salts have two parts. The first part of the name comes from the base. The second part comes from the acid.

Bases are usually metal oxides or hydroxides. The first part of their name tells you which metal, for example:

- **sodium** hydroxide
- **potassium** hydroxide
- **calcium** oxide
- **magnesium** hydroxide
- **copper** oxide
- **iron** oxide.

Acids change their name slightly when they form salts:

- hydrochloric acid gives **chloride** salts
- sulphuric acid gives **sulphate** salts
- nitric acid gives **nitrate** salts.

To name a salt, you take the metal from the base and the changed name from the acid. For example, common salt is made from sodium hydroxide and hydrochloric acid. Its chemical name is therefore **sodium chloride**.

hydrochloric acid + sodium hydroxide ⟶ sodium chloride + water

a
1 Draw a large table like this.

2 Fill in the boxes with the names of the salts. The first row has been done for you.

3 Work out which acids and bases you would need to make the salts in the photographs on the opposite page.

Acid Base	Hydrochloric acid	Sulphuric acid	Nitric acid
Sodium hydroxide	sodium chloride	sodium sulphate	sodium nitrate
Calcium oxide			
Magnesium hydroxide			
Copper oxide			
Iron oxide			
Potassium hydroxide			

What do you know?

1 What chemicals must you mix to make common salt?

2 Copy and complete this word equation:

acid + base ⟶ _____ + _____

3 You could make potassium nitrate by mixing potassium hydroxide with nitric acid.
a What other chemical would be formed?
b Write this reaction as a word equation.

4 Peter was going to make some magnesium nitrate using magnesium hydroxide and nitric acid. Jasmine said he should use magnesium oxide and nitric acid. Who was right?

5 'Alu-ease' indigestion tablets contain aluminium oxide. What salt do they make when they react with your stomach acid?

Key ideas

When an acid reacts with a base, a new chemical called a **salt** is formed.

acid + base ⟶ salt + water

Common salt is a chemical called sodium chloride.

Acids and alkalis

6e Bubbling and fizzing

Another way to neutralise...

Some indigestion tablets contain a chemical called calcium carbonate. This is the chemical that is in limestone.

If calcium carbonate tablets are dropped into acid, the acid is neutralised.

a Look at the picture. What else happens when calcium carbonate reacts with acid?

Getting in a fizz

Carbonates can act like bases. They can neutralise acids. A salt and water are formed as before, but this time there is an extra substance. Bubbles of gas are formed as the carbonate fizzes in the acid. The gas is carbon dioxide.

You can write this as a word equation:

$$\text{acid} + \text{carbonate} \xrightarrow{\text{neutralisation}} \text{salt} + \text{water} + \text{carbon dioxide}$$

So with calcium carbonate in your stomach:

$$\underset{\text{(insoluble)}}{\text{calcium carbonate}} + \text{hydrochloric acid} \rightarrow \underset{\text{(soluble)}}{\text{calcium chloride}} + \text{water} + \underset{\text{(gas)}}{\text{carbon dioxide}}$$

Testing for limestone

Limestone is made of calcium carbonate. It is not always easy to tell limestone from other rocks just by looking at it. Scientists who study rocks often use hydrochloric acid to test the rock.

b 1 How can you use acid to tell if a rock is limestone or not?
   2 Is the rock in the picture limestone? How do you know?

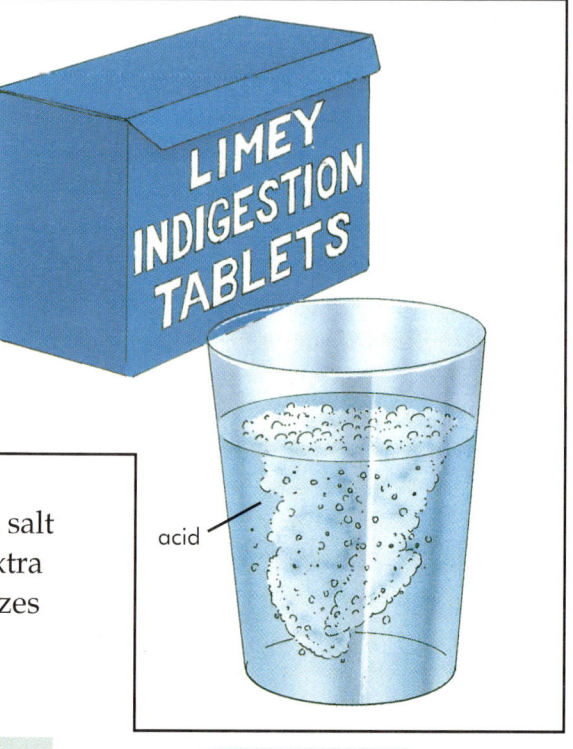

Limescale again

The limescale that forms in kettles and toilets is calcium carbonate. Some toilet limescale removers use hydrochloric acid. The reaction in the toilet is the same as 'Limey' indigestion tablets in your stomach!

Other limescale removers use much weaker acids, such as phosphoric acid.

calcium carbonate + phosphoric acid ⟶ calcium phosphate + water + carbon dioxide

Cola for cleaner kettles?

You might be surprised to find that cola contains phosphoric acid! Don't worry, it is perfectly safe to drink as it is very dilute. But you could descale your kettle if you used a lot of cola.

And next time your younger brother or sister loses a tooth, try leaving it in a glass of cola overnight …

Cola MAX light

2.0 Litre Serve Cool

Ingredients:
Carbonated water, colour (Caramel), Artificial sweetener (Aspartame), Phosphoric acid, flavourings (including Caffeine), preservative (Sodium benzoate), Citric acid.

What do you know?

1 Copy and complete this word equation:

acid + carbonate ⟶ salt + water + _____ _____

2a What is the chemical name for limestone?
b Explain how acid is used to test for limestone.
c What salt forms if you dissolve limestone in hydrochloric acid?

3a What do some limescale removers have in common with cola?
b Arthur liked to swill his diet cola round his teeth, as it felt tingly as it fizzed. He thought this was all right, as diet cola does not contain sugar. After a few weeks he found that his teeth hurt if he had hot drinks or ice lollies. What might have caused his problem?

4 You could use vinegar to descale your kettle. Vinegar is a dilute solution of acetic acid. This acid forms salts called acetates. Write a word equation for this reaction.

Key ideas

Carbonates fizz with acid, giving off carbon dioxide.

The acid is neutralised and a salt and water are also formed.

Limestone fizzes with acid, as it is made of calcium carbonate.

Limescale is also made of calcium carbonate. It can be removed by acids.

Acids and alkalis

6f Acids on the rocks

What's the pH of rain?

Pure water is neutral, with a pH of 7. As rain falls, a little carbon dioxide dissolves in it. This forms a very weak acid solution, with a pH of 6.

Acids can dissolve limestone. When rain falls onto limestone, the limestone slowly dissolves. Cracks in the rock are opened out, and limestone rocks may eventually become riddled with caves.

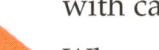

a Where does the dissolved limestone go?

Hard water

Limestone is calcium carbonate. Carbonates usually react with acids to give a salt, carbon dioxide and water. But in the reaction between rainwater and limestone, carbon dioxide is not given off. Instead, a complicated calcium salt is formed. This dissolves in the water.

This salt is carried off in solution. If you live in an area with **hard water**, this chemical is dissolved in your drinking water. It gives the water its taste and is quite good for you.

Getting the limestone back

When you boil hard water, the chemical reaction is reversed. Calcium carbonate is formed again. Calcium carbonate is insoluble in water. It forms solid 'limestone' once more. This is how limescale forms in kettles.

The same thing happens when water evaporates from droplets in a cave. Tiny amounts of limestone are deposited. Over hundreds or thousands of years, these can build up. They make fantastic **stalactites** hanging from the cave roof, with **stalagmites** growing up to meet them from the floor below.

Weathering the rocks

The slightly acidic rainwater also helps to break down other types of rock. Rocks such as granite do not dissolve, but some of the minerals in them slowly break down. This process is called **chemical weathering**. The rocks slowly break down to form **soil**.

Some minerals break down to form clay. This provides important chemicals in the soil, which plants need to grow.

Other minerals, such as quartz (a form of silica), do not react with rainwater. But as the minerals around them break down, they are freed from the rock. They form grains of sand, which collect in the soil or are washed onto beaches.

Granite slowly weathers to sand and clay.

Taking the waters

Rainwater that runs through peaty, boggy areas becomes even more acidic as it picks up chemicals from rotting plants. This more acidic rain can dissolve iron from the rocks. The water in moorland streams is often brown because of this iron. It has a slightly bitter taste.

Some famous springs have iron-rich waters like this. People pay a lot of money to drink the water, because they think it will be good for their health.

b Why might people want to drink iron-rich water? What part of their bodies might it help?

What do you know?

1 Copy and complete the following sentences. Use the words below to fill the gaps.

| solution | carbon dioxide | acidic | dissolve |

Rainwater is slightly _____ because of dissolved _____ _____. Rainwater can slowly _____ limestone. The calcium salts are carried away in _____.

2a Why does some drinking water contain dissolved calcium salts?
b What happens to these salts if the water evaporates or boils?

3 How does the slight acidity of rainwater:
a help plants to grow
b help make sandy beaches?

4 Why are moorland streams often brown?

Key ideas

Rainwater is naturally a very weak acid.

This weak acid reacts with limestone. The reaction forms calcium salts which dissolve in the water.

Water with dissolved calcium salts is called **hard water**.

The reaction is reversed when water boils or evaporates. This makes **stalactites** and **limescale**.

Acids and alkalis

6g Acids and metals

Acids are corrosive. They attack some (but not all) metals, gradually eating them away. What reaction is going on?

Fizzing again!

If you put some zinc pieces into dilute sulphuric acid, it starts to fizz. The tube gets warm, showing that a chemical reaction is taking place. The acid is neutralised and a salt, zinc sulphate, is made. But no water is produced this time, and the gas is hydrogen. You can write this as a word equation:

acid + metal ⟶ salt + hydrogen

For the reaction between zinc and sulphuric acid:

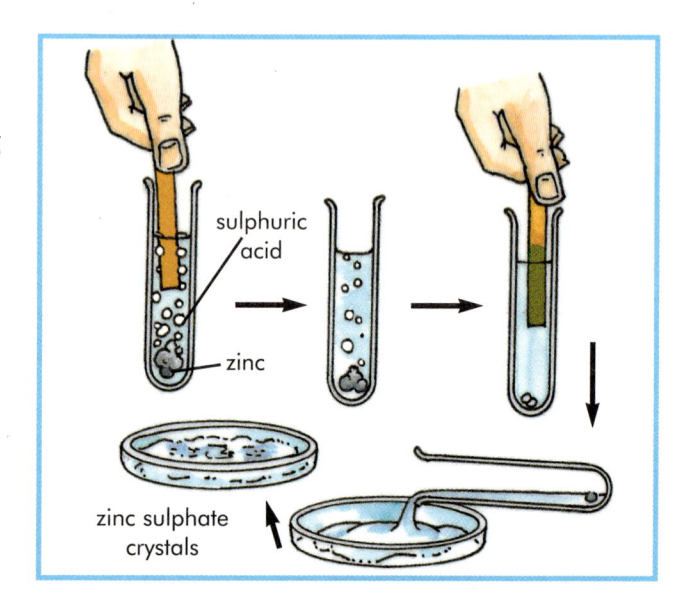

sulphuric acid + zinc ⟶ zinc sulphate + hydrogen

Testing for hydrogen

Hydrogen gas has a low density. It floats up out of an open tube. To test it, you need to trap some gas. You could cover the end of the tube with your thumb until you feel the pressure build up. But remember that strong acid can burn your skin!

Another way of trapping the gas is to pass it through a delivery tube and bubble it up into a tube full of water. This is called **collecting over water**. It is a good way to collect gases that do not dissolve in water.

Once you have trapped some gas, you can test it. If you hold a lighted splint near the open mouth of the tube, you will hear a 'pop' if it is hydrogen. Hydrogen gas burns with a mini-explosion.

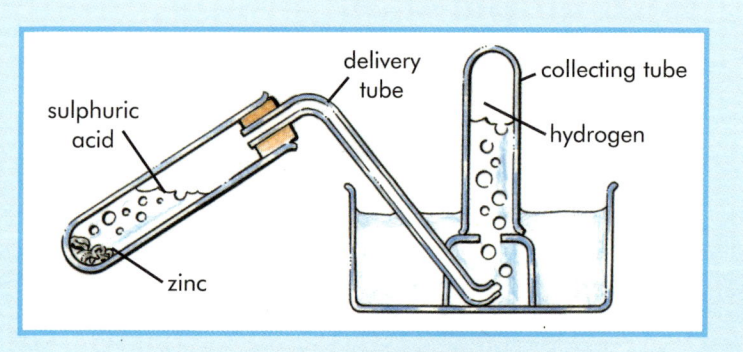

Where does the hydrogen come from?

Many metals react with acid. They all fizz and give off hydrogen. The hydrogen comes from the acid. All acids contain hydrogen. You could think of acids as the 'salts' of hydrogen. For example:

- sulphuric acid is 'hydrogen sulphate'
- hydrochloric acid is 'hydrogen chloride'
- nitric acid is 'hydrogen nitrate'.

When a metal reacts with an acid like this, the metal takes the place of hydrogen in the acid. The metal **displaces** the hydrogen. It is a 'chemical bully'.

Useful hydrogen

Huge amounts of hydrogen are produced by industry every year. Hydrogen is used for all sorts of things, from making fuels to making chocolate!

At the start of the twentieth century, hydrogen was used to fill airships. These airships floated in the air and could carry goods and passengers. But hydrogen burns explosively. It very easily caught fire, with disastrous results. Nowadays, airships use the gas helium. It is not quite so 'light', but it cannot catch fire.

a 1 Why is hydrogen not used to fill airships any more?
2 Which gas is used instead?

The huge airship Hindenberg was destroyed in 1933 when the hydrogen caught fire.

What do you know?

1 Copy and complete this word equation:

acid + metal ⟶ salt + _____

2 Magnesium in hydrochloric acid fizzes and dissolves.
a What is the gas formed?
b Which test shows this?
c What is the salt formed?
d Write a word equation for this reaction.

3 Explain how you could collect some of the gas formed in question **2** over water. Draw a diagram to help you.

4 If you put zinc metal into acid, you always get bubbles of hydrogen, no matter which acid you use.
a Where does this hydrogen come from?
b Describe what happens in the reaction.

Key ideas

All acids contain hydrogen.

Some metals react with acids, pushing out the hydrogen:

acid + metal ⟶ salt + hydrogen

Hydrogen gas pops with a lighted splint.

Hydrogen is 'lighter than air', but it burns very easily.

Acids and alkalis

6 EXTRAS

6b Soap sell

Aunty Mabel gets very confused by all the adverts for cleaning products these days. They baffle her by using scientific terms that she doesn't understand.

1 Write a letter to Aunty Mabel, explaining what the scientific terms mean in these two adverts.

a Buy new **Super Ammonio** for your kitchen!

Its **high pH** formula dissolves away grease.

Get the sparkle without scrubbing!

b You've used ordinary soap all your life. It keeps you clean, but sometimes leaves your skin dry. That's because the *alkaline* formulation of soap can destroy your skin's protective *acid* layer.

Now help is at hand with **Dermata's** new

pH 6 deep cleanser

Its revolutionary soap-free formulation and *low pH* protect your skin's natural defences as it cleans.

6c Ouch!

Stinging nettles are covered with tiny hollow needles full of acid. When you touch a nettle, the needles stick in you and break, injecting this acid into your skin. The acid is strong enough to hurt you, and the area swells up as your body pumps liquid in to 'water down' the acid. Bee stings and ant bites work in a similar way.

Dock leaves contain an alkali. When you crush a dock leaf and rub it onto your nettle rash, this neutralises the acid. It reduces the pain and helps the swelling go down. Dock leaves also help bee stings or ant bites.

1 Explain the science behind using a dock leaf to cure a bee sting.

2 Wasp stings should be treated with vinegar, not dock leaves. What does that tell you about wasp stings?

The stinging hairs of a nettle, magnified about 30 times

6e Baking powder

Baking powder is used to make cakes rise. It contains a weak alkali called sodium bicarbonate, and a weak acid called tartaric acid. These are mixed as dry powders which do not react.

When baking powder is put into cake mixture, it becomes moist. The acid and the alkali start to react. They give off carbon dioxide gas. The gas collects as bubbles inside the cake mixture, and it starts to rise.

Cooking the cake speeds up this reaction, and more bubbles form in the soft mixture. But as the mixture hardens, the bubbles are trapped in place. This gives the cake a delicious light texture.

1 Tartaric acid forms salts called tartrates. Sodium bicarbonate reacts in the same way as sodium carbonate. Write a word equation for the baking powder reaction.

2 Why doesn't the baking powder react when it is dry?

3 Sheila dropped her baking powder pot in the sink and all the powder got damp. She dried it out and it seemed all right, but when she tried to bake a cake with it it did not rise. Why not?

6g Keeping the rain out

Iron rusts in air and water. Iron corrodes even faster in acid, dissolving and giving off hydrogen gas. Rainwater is slightly acidic, so iron will be eaten away by the rain if it is not protected. Factory buildings used to be roofed with corrugated iron, but these roofs corroded away and started to leak in 20 or 30 years.

Lead is much more resistant to acid attack than iron. Slate or tile roofs are often edged with lead 'flashing'. A well leaded roof might last for over 100 years.

Copper is even more resistant as it is much less reactive than iron or lead. Copper does not react with acids to give hydrogen gas. Some buildings such as churches have copper roofs that have lasted for centuries. The golden brown of the copper metal becomes a beautiful green surface.

The only metals that are completely unaffected by acids are precious metals such as gold or platinum. But even if they weren't so expensive, they would be too soft to make a decent roof!

1 Why do corrugated iron roofs need to be painted or covered with tar?

2 What is unusual about the reaction when copper is corroded by an acid?

3 Why are gold and platinum so prized as metals, even though they are too soft for most uses?

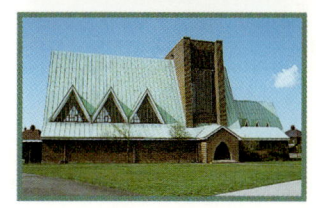

Using food

7a All cut up

We use the wood from a tree in many different ways. But before we can use the tree, we have to cut it up into smaller pieces.

a Think of five different uses of wood. How many of them need the wood to be cut up first?

In the same way, our food is not much use to our bodies in the form that we eat it. We need food for our body cells to respire to give them energy. Food also provides our cells with materials for growth and repair. But an apple, a burger or a biscuit can't travel round your body in the blood. Even if they could, your cells couldn't use them!

What's in food?

Our food contains **carbohydrates**, **proteins** and **fats**, as well as vitamins, minerals, fibre and water. This table shows how we take in and use some of these food substances in our bodies.

Food substance	Foods that contain it	Use in the body
carbohydrate	cakes, bread, potatoes, biscuits, pasta, rice	energy from respiration, for movement, growth, reproduction, keeping warm and all our body processes
protein	meat, fish, cheese, milk, beans, lentils	building new cells and repairing damaged ones
fat	cream, oils, butter and margarine, cakes	energy from respiration storing food for energy

Digestion

Before your food can be used in your body, it has to be broken down into smaller and smaller pieces. This is **digestion**. It takes place in a long tube with special organs connected to it called your **digestive system**.

First the food is chopped up small so it is easier to swallow. This is what your teeth are for.

After the food has been chewed up, the large molecules in carbohydrates, proteins and fats are broken down chemically. They are split into much smaller molecules. These small molecules can be used by your cells.

Teeth come in different sizes and shapes. They chop, slice or crunch food into smaller pieces.

What do you know?

1 Answer these questions, using complete sentences.
a Why do we need food?
b What are the three main substances contained in our food?
c What must happen to our food before it can be useful to our bodies?

2 Write out these sentences, putting the correct pairs together.

Protein	supplies energy.
Bread and rice	stores energy.
Fat	is used for growth and repair.
Carbohydrate	contain protein.
Meat and fish	contain carbohydrate.

3 Look at the teeth in the photographs. What do the teeth tell you about the food each animal eats?

Key ideas

Food contains **carbohydrates**, **fats** and **proteins**. These provide cells with energy and with materials for growth and repair.

To be useful in the body, food needs to be broken down into smaller molecules. This breaking down is **digestion**.

Using food

7b The digestion machine

Your digestive system is like a factory conveyor belt. Food travels along the gut, getting broken down at various points. Small useful molecules are sent to the cells of the body, and any food that is undigested is passed out at the other end.

▶ a   How do you think the food is moved along the gut conveyor belt?

Into the mouth

Food comes into your digestive system through your mouth. But even after you have swallowed the food, it is not really inside your body! Your gut is a tube 8–9 m long which runs from your mouth to your anus. Food doesn't really get into your body until it passes through the gut walls into the blood.

In your mouth, your teeth start to break up the food into smaller pieces. Your mouth also produces **saliva**. This is a liquid which makes your food easier to swallow. It also starts the chemical breakdown of some of your food.

Down the hatch

Once you have swallowed your food, it is moved steadily along your gut. Muscles squeeze to keep the food moving and to mix it to a paste. The muscles contract and relax in waves and this is called **peristalsis**.

The job of the gut is to break down your food into small molecules. These can be taken into your blood and carried to the cells of your body. The gut has different parts, each doing a different job. The whole gut is coiled into your abdomen, the bit of your body below your ribs.

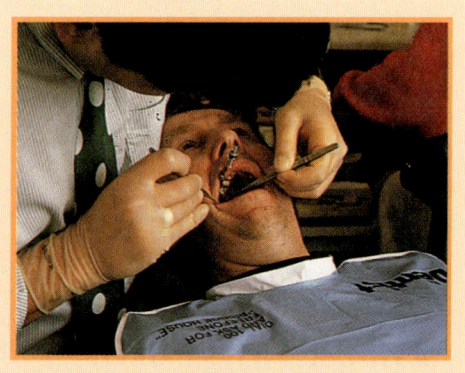

Microbes live on the food left on your teeth. They produce acids as waste. The acids make holes in your teeth, and work for your dentist!

Peristalsis is like squeezing a toothpaste tube!

Gut feeling

The chewed food is swallowed and goes into the oesophagus. This is a muscular tube which can squeeze food down to the stomach in 7 seconds.

Your stomach is a muscular bag containing acidic juices. It stores food for about 3–4 hours, squidging it up and breaking down protein. From here, the partly digested paste is squirted into the small intestine.

The liver and pancreas make juices which are squirted into the small intestine. These help break down the food in the small intestine.

It takes food about 6 hours to travel along the 6 m length of your small intestine. The final breakdown of the food takes place here. The small food molecules are absorbed (taken into your blood through your gut wall).

All your undigested food such as fibre collects in the large intestine. Water is removed back into your body to leave a thick waste sludge. This is passed out through the anus.

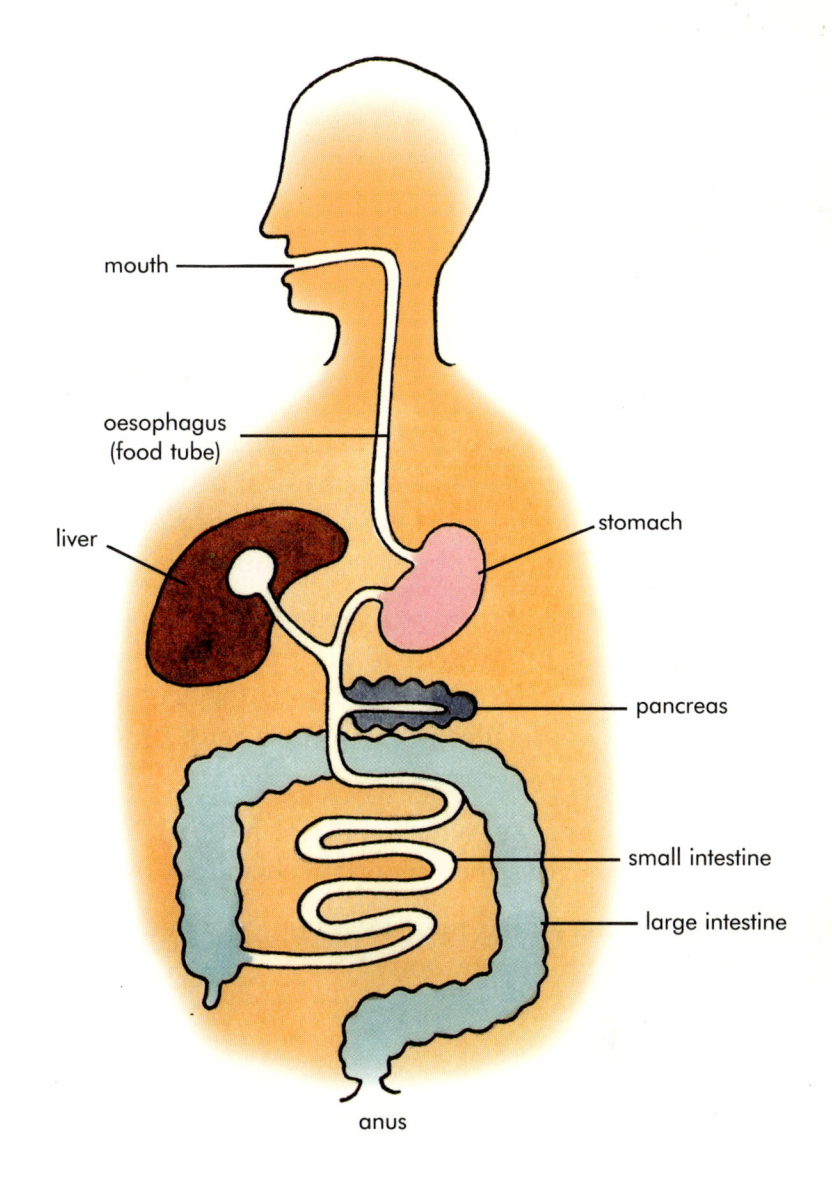

What do you know?

1 Write these sentences in the correct order.
a Waste material passes out through the anus.
b Food enters the gut through the mouth where it is chopped into smaller pieces by the teeth.
c In the small intestine, digestion is completed and the digested food is absorbed into the blood.
d After swallowing, food is moved along the gut by peristalsis.
e It enters the stomach, which is a muscular bag of acidic juices for digesting protein.
f In the large intestine, water is removed from the undigested remains of the food.

2a Why is saliva important in the digestion of food?
b Why is it important to clean your teeth regularly?

Key ideas

The digestive system is a muscular tube running through the body.

Food is moved through the gut by muscles squeezing in **peristalsis**.

Using food

7c The breakdown gang

Your teeth cut up your food into smaller pieces. They greatly increase the surface area of your food before you swallow it, which makes it easier to break down. Cutting up the food is a **physical** process. But most of the digestion of your food takes place further down your gut, and it is a **chemical** process.

If you put a piece of meat in a beaker of acid and leave it for several days, it will disappear! The large protein molecules are broken down by the acid into much smaller molecules called **amino acids**. These then dissolve.

Your stomach is a bag which contains hydrochloric acid. It also contains other important chemicals.

a What problems would there be if you only had acid to digest protein in your body?

Enzymes

The parts of the gut make different chemicals which help the breakdown of carbohydrates, proteins and fats. These chemicals are called **enzymes**. An enzyme speeds up a chemical reaction. Food molecules break down slowly in acids and other substances, but it would take far too long to be any use to your body. Enzymes make things happen much more quickly.

The enzymes in your gut let you break down your food in a few hours instead of several days.

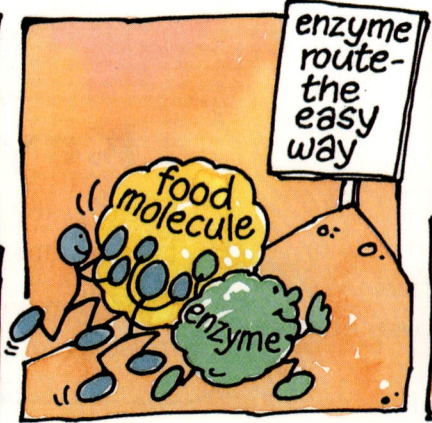

Chemical breakdown

Your pancreas makes lots of enzymes, and so does your small intestine. These enzymes speed up the breakdown of proteins, carbohydrates and fats. They produce smaller, simpler molecules which can pass into the blood.

The physical chewing of your teeth and the squidging of the gut muscles give your food a very big surface for the enzymes to work on. This means they can do their job of chemical breakdown much faster.

Not everything you eat is broken down by enzymes. Some substances simply can't be digested because you don't have the enzymes to do it. Others don't need any digestion because they are already small molecules. Minerals and vitamins are not broken down because they can be taken directly into the blood and sent to the cells where they are needed.

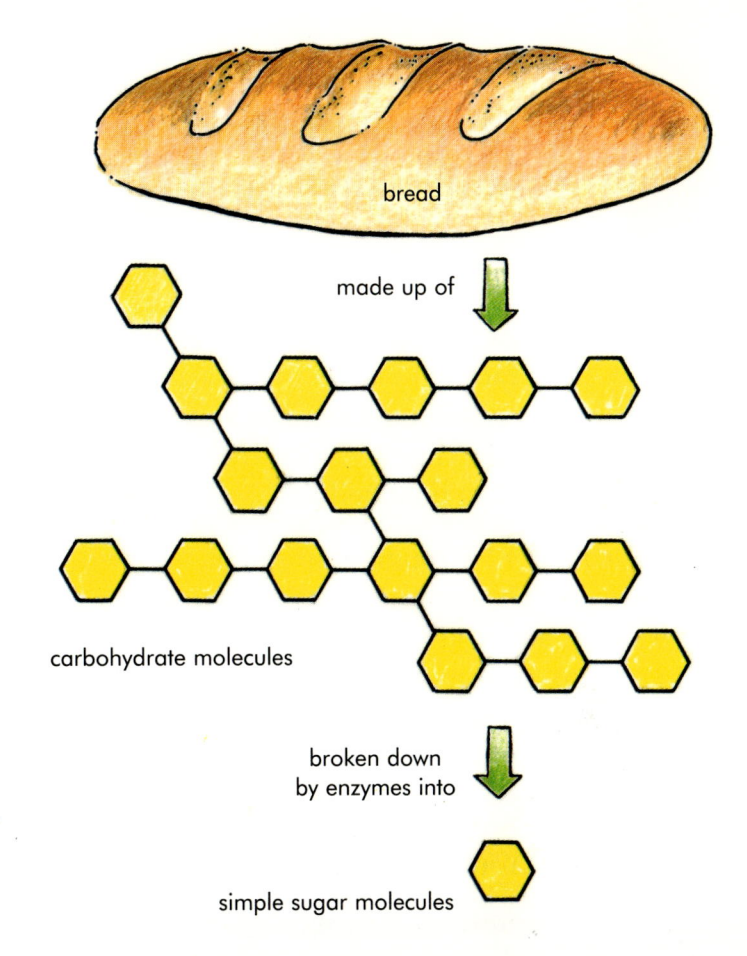

bread

made up of

carbohydrate molecules

broken down by enzymes into

simple sugar molecules

What do you know?

1 Copy and complete the following sentences. Use the words below to fill the gaps.

| teeth | enzymes | broken down |
| quickly | surface | gut |

The food we eat needs to be _____ _____ into small molecules before it can be used in the body. Your _____ and the muscles of your _____ physically break your food into small pieces. This gives a big _____. The chemical breakdown of your food is done by _____. They make reactions happen _____.

2 A piece of bread contains carbohydrates, proteins and some vitamins and minerals. Your body treats the carbohydrates and proteins differently from the minerals and vitamins. How?

3 Here are two sayings about digestion. Can you give a scientific explanation for them?
a Chew every mouthful of food 30 times before swallowing.
b A noisy gut is a healthy gut.

Key ideas

Different parts of the gut make different **enzymes** which help the breakdown of carbohydrates, proteins and fats.

An **enzyme** speeds up a chemical reaction by making it easier for it to happen.

Using food

7d Keep the best

Can you guess what this picture shows? No, it's not a nightmare in a rubber glove factory! This is a highly magnified picture of the lining of your small intestine. The strange finger-like **villi** make sure that all the digested food molecules get into your blood, to be carried to your cells.

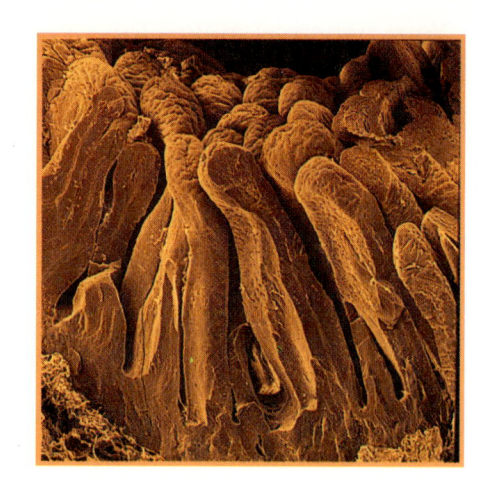

As food is squeezed through your gut, it is mixed with several litres of digestive juices. These contain enzymes to break down the food. The process is rather noisy, and you can sometimes hear the rumbles and gurgles made by your gut! As your meal moves along your small intestine, all that is left is a chemical soup. You need some parts of the soup, but not all of it. Your body needs to sort out which is which. This is where the villi come in.

> **a** Try this exercise. You will need a piece of cotton or string.
>
> **1** Measure the distance in a straight line between points A and B, and the distance between points C and D. Note them down.
>
> **2** Measure the length of the line joining A and B, and the length of the line joining C and D.
>
> **3** What is the effect of the villi?

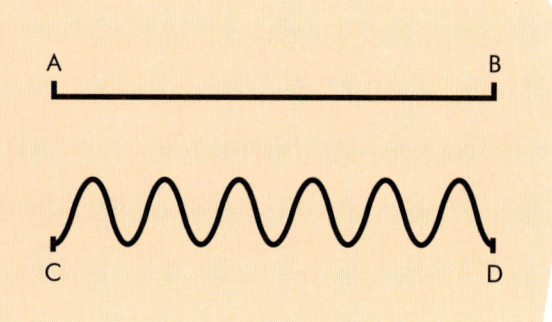

Taking it all in

The villi give the small intestine a much bigger surface than if it was a smooth tube. Villi have a blood supply and thin walls. This means that the digested food molecules can easily pass through into the blood. We say they have been **absorbed**. Once in the blood, they are carried to the liver and then off round the body.

Big molecules, bits of undigested food and micro-organisms which live in the gut can't be absorbed by the villi. They are left in the small intestine.

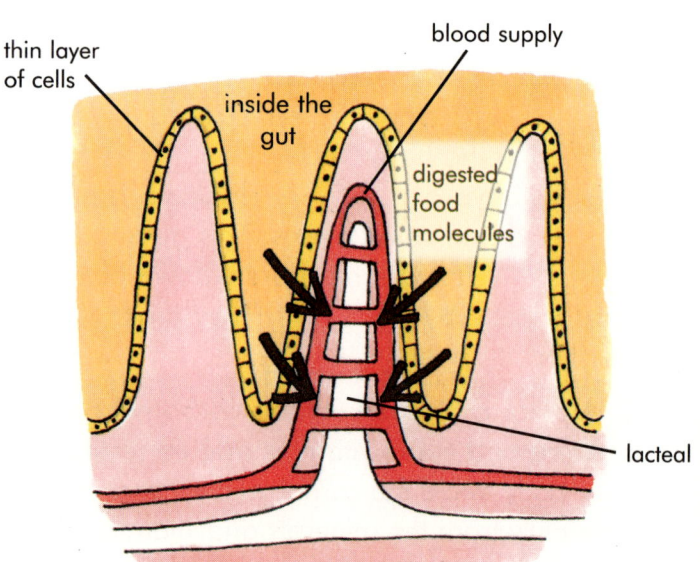

100

Getting rid of the rest

All the useful digested food is absorbed into the blood in the small intestine. A thin, watery liquid is left inside. This is squeezed along to the large intestine, which is the waste disposal unit of the body. No digestion takes place in the large intestine, but much of the water is absorbed back into the body.

▶ **b** Where do you think all the water has come from?

What is left is semi-solid waste called **faeces**. It is made up of food that can't be digested (like fibre), lots of dead gut cells and micro-organisms. It will also contain any fingernails, fruit pips or other things which you might accidentally swallow.

When your large intestine gets full, messages go to your brain and you pass the faeces out of your body through a ring of muscle called your **anus**. This process is called **egestion**.

The waste from a meal should leave your body within about 24 hours if your gut is working well. If you are constipated, waste stays in the large intestine far too long. Almost all the water is removed, making the faeces dry and hard.

If you have diarrhoea, your large intestine is irritated. Waste is not held there long enough for the water to be reabsorbed. More children in the world die of diarrhoea than any other disease, because water is lost from the body so fast.

There are lots of treatments for constipation, but more fibre in the diet is the best solution.

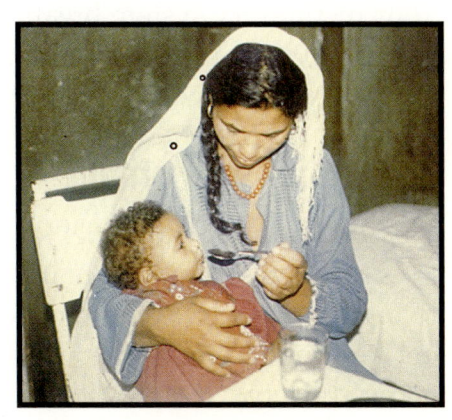

In diarrhoea, the water, and the minerals it carries with it, need to be replaced quickly.

What do you know?

1 Write these sentences in the correct order to explain what happens to food in your small and large intestines.

a The waste material is egested from the body through the anus.
b Digestion is finished in the small intestine, giving a chemical soup of useful molecules.
c Water is absorbed from the waste in the large intestine, leaving semi-solid faeces.
d Once the useful molecules have been absorbed, the watery waste is squeezed into the large intestine.
e The villi give the lining of the small intestine a very big surface.
f The products of digestion are absorbed into the blood through the villi of the small intestine.

2 Young children often suffer from constipation or diarrhoea. Design a leaflet for your doctor's surgery explaining to parents what happens in the large intestine. Include what happens when it works properly, and what goes wrong in these common illnesses.

Key ideas

The lining of the small intestine is covered by **villi** to give a large surface.

The small useful molecules produced by digestion are **absorbed** from the small intestine into the bloodstream.

Water is reabsorbed in the large intestine. Waste material is **egested** as **faeces**.

Using food

7e Using what you've got

Your body has systems to make sure that plenty of food and oxygen reach the cells of your body. Your digestive system breaks down the food you eat into small, soluble molecules such as glucose. Your respiratory system breathes air into the body and takes in oxygen in your lungs. Your circulatory (blood) system transports the food and oxygen to your cells. But what do they do with it?

Energy for everything

The food you eat is the fuel for your body. Lots of reactions take place in your body, to repair damaged cells, to make new cells and to produce chemicals. These reactions all need energy. **Respiration** takes place in cells to make the energy from your food available for the body.

Respiration is the reaction between glucose and the oxygen you breathe in. This reaction produces energy for the cell, and carbon dioxide and water as waste products.

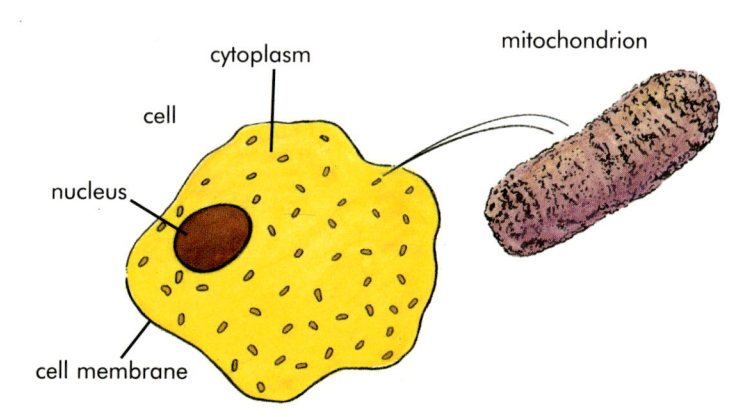

Respiration takes place in **mitochondria**. Mitochondria are found in every cell in your body.

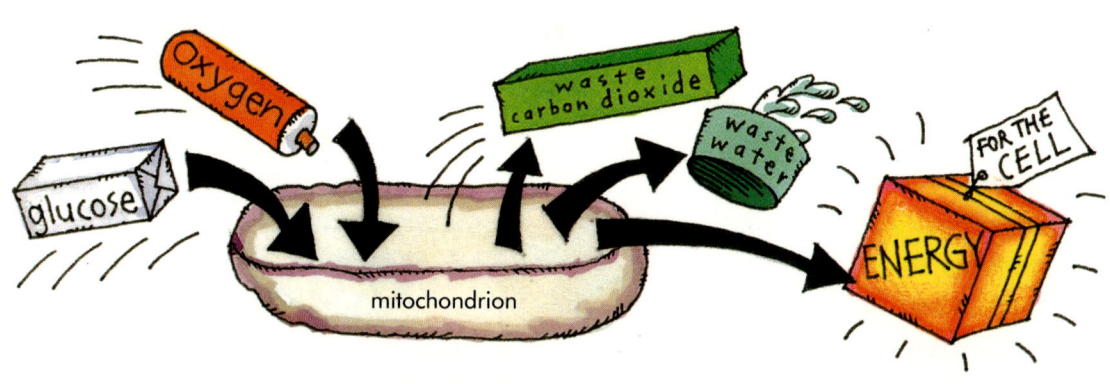

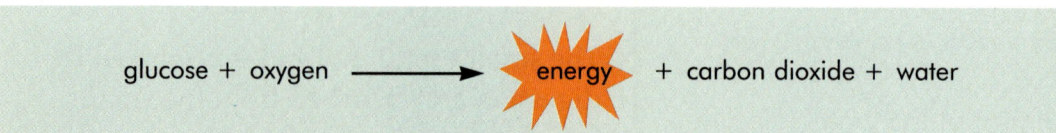

glucose + oxygen ⟶ energy + carbon dioxide + water

Respiration takes place with the help of special enzymes found only on the membranes inside the mitochondria.

Not just for you

Respiration provides our cells with all the energy they need. But other living organisms need energy too. Where does it come from?

a Write down how each of these living things gets its food and oxygen.

Different organisms may get their food and oxygen in different ways. But all living things get energy from food in the same way. Plant and animal cells all contain mitochondria, and they all carry out respiration. In every organism, glucose and oxygen react together to give energy, carbon dioxide and water.

What do you know?

1 Write these sentences in the best order to explain how cells release energy from food.
a Carbon dioxide and water are the waste products of the reaction.
b Energy is made available to the cells of all living things during respiration.
c We get our oxygen by breathing and our glucose from digested food.
d Respiration takes place in the mitochondria of the cells.
e In respiration, glucose and oxygen react together to provide energy for the cell.

2 Respiration takes place in all living cells. Why is it so important?

3a What are mitochondria?
b Inside the mitochondria are lots of folded membranes. These give a very big surface area. Why do you think this is important to the way the mitochondria work?

Key ideas

Respiration releases the energy in food so that the cell can use it.

glucose + oxygen ⟶ energy + carbon dioxide + water

Respiration takes place in the **mitochrondria** of the cells of all living things.

103

Using food
7 EXTRAS

7b Guess the gut!

The length of an animal's gut depends on two things. One is the size of the animal. There is a limit to how much you can fit inside a mouse! The other is the diet eaten by the animal. All plant tissue contains cellulose which is difficult for most animals to digest. They do not make the enzyme **cellulase** which breaks down the cellulose cell wall of the plant cells. The cell wall protects the plant cell from digestion. So herbivores need a very long gut. However, animal tissue is mainly protein with some fat, and there are no cell walls to break down, so it is much easier to digest. Carnivores don't need a very long gut.

1 Look at the bar chart. The bars represent a human being, a cheetah and a pony. Which bar fits which animal? Explain why you made your choices.

2 Many herbivores, such as cows and termites, have special micro-organisms in their guts. Because of these micro-organisms, their guts can be shorter than they would otherwise be. How do you think the micro-organisms help the herbivores cope with their food?

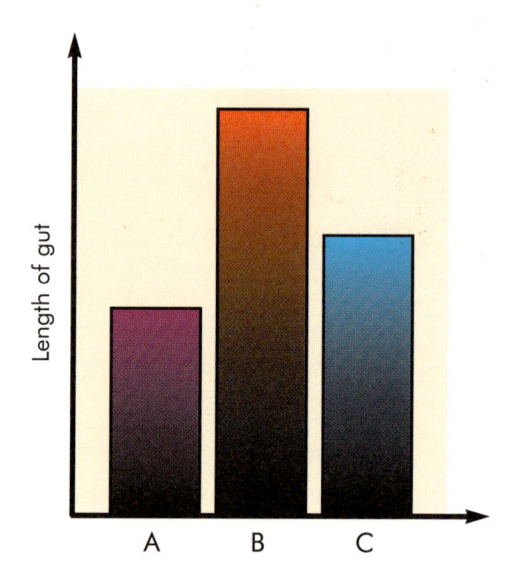

3 Rabbits have to eat their food twice to break it down. After they have eaten grass, they produce lots of soft faeces. They eat these and re-digest them before producing the dry 'rabbit droppings' we all recognise. What does this tell you about the gut of a rabbit?

4 The amount of faeces produced by an animal tells us how much of its food is not digested. Sketch a bar chart showing the amount of faeces you think would be produced by three animals of similar size:

a a carnivore
b a herbivore
c an omnivore (like people) which eats both plants and animals.

7c Amylase, the starch digester

One of the most common carbohydrates is starch, which is found in flour and potatoes. The chemical breakdown of starch begins before you even swallow your food, because the saliva in your mouth contains an enzyme called **amylase**. Amylase breaks down starch into glucose. If you put a piece of bread in your mouth and chew it for several minutes you will notice that it begins to taste sweet. Starch doesn't taste sweet, but glucose does.

If iodine solution is added to starch solution, a blue-black colour appears. If iodine is added to a solution which contains no starch, the iodine stays yellowy brown.

Here is an experiment to show how amylase works on starch. In the experiment, iodine was used to show when the amylase had broken down all the starch.

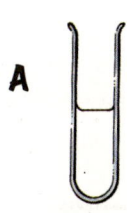

A Amylase and starch solutions are mixed together and put in the fridge.

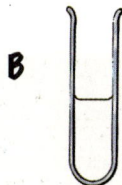

Samples of the mixture from the fridge are mixed with iodine every 5 minutes until no blue-black colour appears.

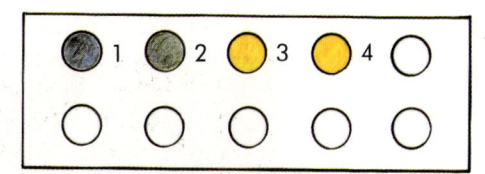

B Amylase and starch solutions are mixed together and kept at body temperature.

Samples of the mixture at body temperature are mixed with iodine every 5 minutes until no blue-black colour appears.

1 How many minutes did it take for the amylase to break down all the starch when it was kept in the fridge?

2 How long did it take the amylase to break down all the starch when it was kept at body temperature?

3 What does this tell you about the way amylase works?

4 How could you change this experiment to find out what happens to amylase in the acidic conditions of the stomach? Remember to make it a fair test.

5 What do you predict will happen in your changed experiment?

Speed

8a Travelling fast

We can see when something is moving quickly, because it looks blurred. The train in the photograph is moving at high speed.

a How can you tell that the train is moving quickly? How can you tell that the rails are not moving?

The photograph of the gymnast was taken with a special camera. The camera has a flashgun which flashes several times in a second.

You can see how the gymnast has moved. When he is moving slowly, the pictures are close together. When he is moving fast, the pictures are further apart.

b When was the gymnast moving quickly? When was he moving slowly?

106

Racing along

In the 100-metre race, everyone runs the same distance. The officials have stopwatches for measuring the time each runner takes. The person who takes the shortest time is the winner.

c Whose speed was the highest in the race? Whose speed was the lowest?

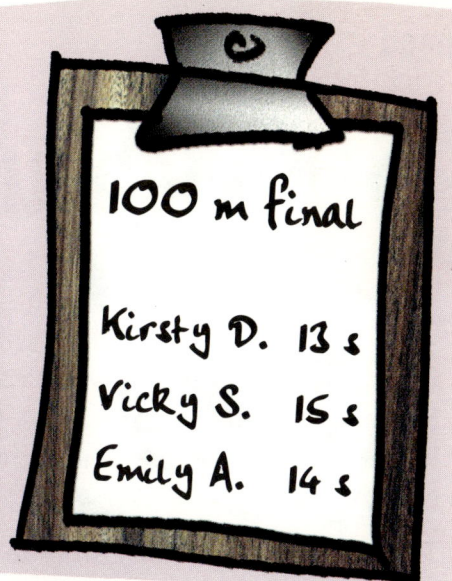

100 m final
Kirsty D. 13 s
Vicky S.   15 s
Emily A.   14 s

In the Le Mans 24-hour race, the drivers have to drive as far as possible in 24 hours. The driver who travels furthest in the time has the highest speed.

d Arturo Antonioni travelled 4600 km in 24 hours. Benito Bruni travelled 4450 km in the same time. Who had the higher speed, Arturo or Benito?

What do you know?

1 Copy and complete the following sentence. Use the words below to fill the gaps. There are two correct answers! Can you find them both?

| high | low | long | short |

If you travel a _____ distance in a _____ time, then your speed is _____.

2 In cartoon films, characters like Tom and Jerry often run fast.
How do they show this in the film?

3 Imagine a typical school day. Sometimes you are moving quickly, sometimes slowly. Write the things in the list in order, from fastest to slowest.

- walking into school in the morning
- walking out of school at the end of the day
- lying in bed before the alarm sounds
- travelling on the bus to school
- playing hockey during Games
- cycling along the road to see your friend

Key ideas

Your **speed** tells you how fast you are moving. If you travel a long distance in a short time, your speed is high.

Speed

8b Measuring speed

Car drivers need to know the car's speed, to make sure they do not break the speed limit. The speedometer shows how fast the car is travelling.

The police use a radar gun to tell how fast a car is travelling. They will stop anyone who is going too fast.

a What is the highest speed a car is permitted to travel at on Britain's roads?

Measuring speed

To work out the speed of a runner, we need to know two things:

- the distance she moves
- the time she takes.

The tape measure is used to measure the distance she runs, and the stopwatch times how long she takes.

Calculating speed

We can calculate her speed using this formula:

$$\text{speed} = \frac{\text{distance moved}}{\text{time taken}}$$

In Science, we have to be careful about the units we use. The table shows the correct units.

Quantity	Unit	Symbol for unit
distance moved	metres	m
time taken	seconds	s
speed	metres per second	m/s

Personal best

Mary has managed her fastest run yet. She ran 80 m in 10 s. Now we can calculate her speed:

$$\text{speed} = \frac{80 \text{ m}}{10 \text{ s}} = 8 \text{ m/s}$$

b Carl is Mary's younger brother. He took 16 s to run 80 m. What was his speed during the race?

Light gates

You can use **light gates** to measure the speed of a moving trolley or car. When the trolley passes the first gate, it breaks a light beam and the clock starts. When it passes the second gate, the clock stops. This tells you how long the trolley took to travel from the first gate to the second.

c What else must you measure to find the trolley's speed?

A computer can work out the speed for you.

What do you know?

1 Nicky got a bit confused about the correct way to calculate speed. He wrote down three different formulas. Copy out the correct one.

$$\text{speed} = \text{distance} \times \text{time}$$

$$\text{speed} = \frac{\text{distance}}{\text{time}}$$

$$\text{speed} = \frac{\text{time}}{\text{distance}}$$

2 The Flying Scotsman travels 600 km from Edinburgh to London in 4 hours. What is its speed, in kilometres per hour, for the journey?

3 On sports day, John ran 400 m in 50 s. Jane ran 1500 m in 250 s. Who was faster, and what was their speed?

Key ideas

To find the speed of something, we have to measure the distance it moves and the time it takes.

To calculate the speed of something, we use:

$$\text{speed} = \frac{\text{distance moved}}{\text{time taken}}$$

In Science, speed is measured in m/s (metres per second).

109

Speed

8c Faster and slower

A speedway bike has a very powerful engine, but it has no brakes. The rider turns the front wheel sideways if he wants to slow down. Lots of dust flies up in the air.

a What force makes the speedway bike slow down?

Downhill all the way

This toboggan is sliding down a slope. It goes faster and faster.

b What force pulls the toboggan down the slope?

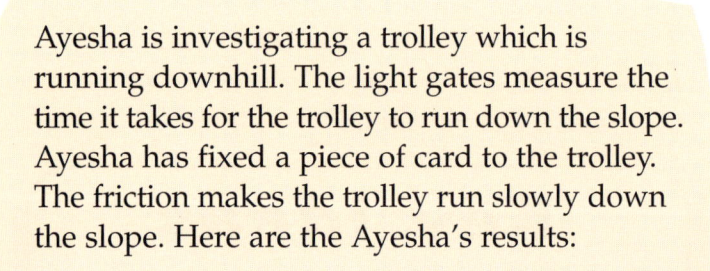

Ayesha is investigating a trolley which is running downhill. The light gates measure the time it takes for the trolley to run down the slope. Ayesha has fixed a piece of card to the trolley. The friction makes the trolley run slowly down the slope. Here are the Ayesha's results:

time for trolley to run down slope = 4 s

length of slope = 2 m

c What is the trolley's speed down the slope?

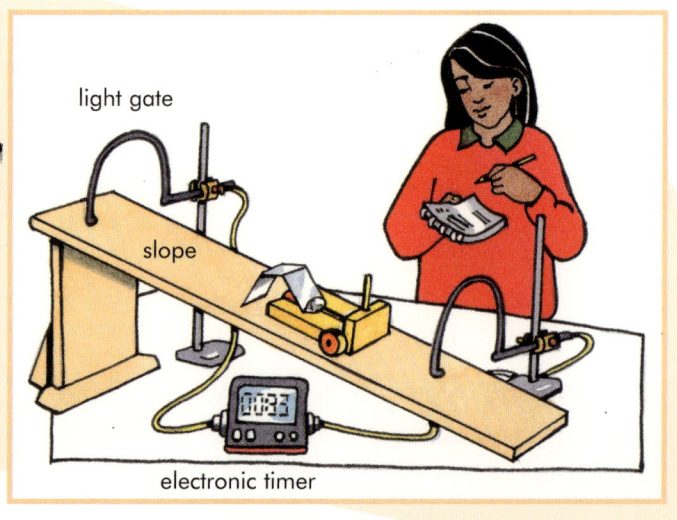

110

Unbalanced forces

The car driver wants to go faster, to overtake the lorry. For the car to go faster, the force of the engine must be bigger than the force of air resistance. The forces must be **unbalanced** to increase its speed.

Now the driver wants to go slower, because the traffic lights ahead are red. She puts on the brakes so that the force of friction on the car is greater than the force of the engine. The forces must be **unbalanced** to decrease its speed.

air resistance   force of engine

air resistance + force of brakes   force of engine

d Draw a force diagram to show the forces on a speedway rider who is slowing down. Remember to label the force arrows.

What do you know?

1 Copy and complete the following sentences. Use the words below to fill the gaps. You can use words more than once.

| balanced | friction | unbalanced | gravity |

The force of _____ can make it difficult for something to travel fast.

Things fall faster and faster when they are pulled downwards by the force of _____.

For something to go faster, the forces on it must be _____.

For something to go slower, the forces on it must be _____.

2 Jo dropped a stone down a deep well. The picture shows how far the stone had fallen after 1 s, 2 s and 3 s.

a What is happening to the speed of the stone as it falls?
b How can you tell?
c Draw a diagram to show the force of gravity acting on the stone.
d What is another name for the force of gravity on the stone?

Key ideas

To increase or decrease your speed, you need **unbalanced** forces.

If the forces on you are unbalanced, your speed will change.

111

Speed

8 EXTRAS

8a At the movies

A cinema film is made up of lots of separate photographs. Twenty-four frames are shown every second. The picture changes slightly from one frame to the next. To our eyes, it looks like continuous movement.

1 Draw a series of frames to show a car driving at a steady speed past a person who is not moving. Explain how you have shown a steady speed.

2 Draw a series of frames to show a car speeding up as it leaves the traffic lights. Explain your drawing.

8b Cross-country run

Hamid is a cross-country runner. He is training for the championships. The picture shows his daily practice run. He starts his stopwatch, and notes the time at the end of each section of the run.

1 Copy and complete the table.

Section of run	Distance run (m)	Time taken (s)	Speed (m/s)
across fields	2000	400	
up hill	1200	400	
through woods	2000	500	

2a How long did Hamid take to do the whole run?

b How far did he run?

c What was Hamid's average speed for the whole run?

8b Catching the train

It is 24 km from Dewsbury to Wednesbury. There are three trains a day. The timetable shows when they run.

1a Which train is quickest?

b What is its speed?

	Train A	Train B	Train C
Dewsbury dep	08:10	13:00	17:50
Wednesbury arr	08:28	13:16	18:10

8c Balanced forces

When the forces on a car are balanced, it moves at a steady speed. The pictures show the forces on a car at different stages of its journey.

A The car is waiting to set off.

B The car is moving off.

C The car is moving fast.

D The driver is braking.

1 In the first picture, are the forces balanced or unbalanced?

2a In **B**, which force is bigger?

b How does the car's speed change?

3a In **C**, the two arrows are the same length. What does this tell you about the forces on the car?

b Is the car speeding up, slowing down, or continuing at a steady speed?

4 What can you say about the forces and about the car's speed in **D**?

Chemicals in action

9a Chemicals you need

Then ...

Everything in the world is made from chemicals, and that includes you! Ancient people used chemicals just as they found them, without changing them. They used plants and animals for food, animal skins for clothing, wood for burning, rocks for tools and caves for shelters.

... and now

Today, most of the things that we use have been changed from their natural state. We purify some things, like salt and sugar, using physical processes. Some clothes are made of purified natural materials, such as cotton or wool. We make other things, like plastics, using chemical reactions. We change **raw materials** to produce things that are useful to us.

Buildings are made from brick or concrete. These materials are made from rocks, by chemical processes.

Some clothes are made of synthetic materials, such as nylon or polyester. These synthetic materials are made from crude oil, by chemical processes.

Microwave and electric ovens run on electricity. This is produced by burning fuels in power stations.

Cooking is a chemical process. Some food comes ready cooked. It contains chemical preservatives to stop it going bad before you eat it.

More and more products

Nearly everything you use has been produced using chemical reactions to change raw materials.

Plastics are made from crude oil.

Glass is made from sand and other chemicals.

Many medicines and cosmetics are made from crude oil.

Ceramics are made from clay.

Bleach is made from sea water.

Rubber is made from plants or from crude oil and sulphur.

Metals such as iron and steel are made from metal ores found in the rocks.

What are they made from?

a

1 Draw a table like this on a full page.

2 In the first column, list all the materials shown in the picture above.

3 In the second column, write down the raw materials they are made from.

4 Add other things that you use to your table.

Materials used	Raw materials

What do you know?

1 Copy and complete the following sentences. Use the words below to fill the gaps.

| reactions | chemicals | raw materials |

Everything is made from _____. Many natural substances are used as _____ _____ to make other things. This usually involves making new chemicals through chemical _____.

2 People need food, clothing, heat and shelter. Think about how people get these four things now, and how cave people used to get them. Write notes showing how things have changed.

Key ideas

Everything is made of chemicals.

Natural substances can be used as **raw materials** to make the things you use.

Most industrial processes involve chemical reactions.

Chemicals in action

9b Ringing the changes

There and back

Some raw materials are changed using **physical processes**. Physical processes are easily reversed. For example, crude oil is distilled to make products such as petrol.

Crude oil is a black liquid found underground. It is a mixture of useful liquids. To get it out, oil companies drill oil wells. The crude oil comes up to the surface through pipes. To distil it, they heat the oil to turn it into a gas. Then they cool it to condense it again. The liquids each condense separately.

a Table salt is made from rock salt. Which reversible physical process is used to do this?

Drilling for oil in the rocks under the North Sea

One-way street

Most of the things you use are made using **chemical reactions**. For example, crude oil is used to make plastics such as polythene and PVC. These chemical processes are not reversible.

Most chemical reactions are one-way like this.

crude oil —chemical processes→ plastics

You can't turn an old record collection back into crude oil!

Off they go

Some chemical reactions are easier to get going than others. Some chemicals react as soon as you mix them. It's harder to make plastics. You need to get the conditions just right.

Acids and bases react easily. The 'one-way sign' on this reaction is very clear.

acid + base —one-way only→ salt + water

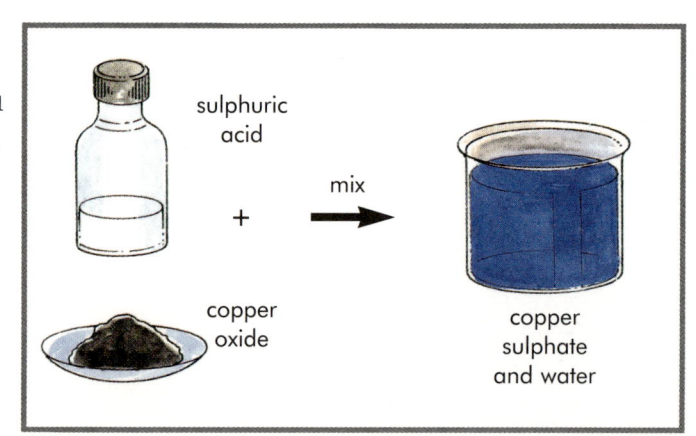

sulphuric acid + copper oxide —mix→ copper sulphate and water

116

Give it a kick

Dry wood burns. It reacts with oxygen. But you can leave dry wood surrounded by air and nothing happens. Why?

The reaction needs a 'kick-start' of energy to get it going. If you heat the wood enough, it will start to burn. Once it is burning, the chemical reaction gives out heat and light energy. The one-way reaction continues.

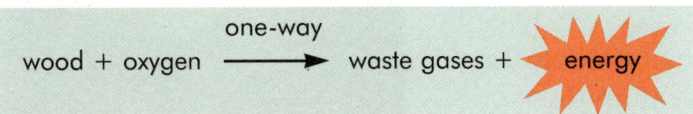

wood + oxygen —one-way→ waste gases + energy

It just needs a 'kick' to get the reaction started.

Writing word equations

To write a word equation, you need to know:
- What chemicals do you start with? (the **reactants**)
- What new chemicals form? (the **products**)

You write the reactants on the left and the products on the right. The arrow shows the one-way direction of the reaction. You can write the name of the process, such as 'burning', above the arrow.

reactants ——→ products

Example: When natural gas burns, it reacts with the oxygen in the air. Carbon dioxide and water vapour are formed.

First sort out the reactants and products as in the table. Then write them in the word equation:

Reactants	Products
natural gas	carbon dioxide
oxygen	water

natural gas + oxygen —burning→ carbon dioxide + water

What do you know?

1 If you put magnesium ribbon into sulphuric acid, it starts to fizz. Hydrogen gas and magnesium sulphate are formed.
a Is this a physical or chemical change?
b Did this reaction need a 'kick-start'?
c Write a word equation for this reaction.

2 Gunpowder contains carbon, sulphur and a source of oxygen. Sulphur burns in air to form sulphur dioxide.
a When gunpowder explodes, is it a physical or chemical change?
b Why can you store fireworks full of gunpowder safely?
c What compound forms when carbon reacts with oxygen?
d Write a word equation for the reaction when gunpowder explodes.

Key ideas

Physical changes are reversible.

Most **chemical changes** are one-way reactions. They cannot easily be reversed.

The **reactants** are the chemicals that react. The **products** are the chemicals that are formed.

Some reactions happen as soon as the reactants mix. Others need a 'kick-start' of energy.

Word equations are a short way of describing chemical reactions.

117

Chemicals in action

9c Fossil sunshine

Many chemical reactions give out energy. This energy may be in the form of heat, light or electricity. We use some reactions to give us this energy, rather than to give us the chemical products.

Fuels contain stored chemical energy. The energy is released when they burn. Burning is the chemical reaction between a fuel and the oxygen in the air. Burning is also called **combustion**.

$$\text{fuel} + \text{oxygen} \xrightarrow{\text{combustion}} \text{waste gases} + \text{energy}$$

Combustion is a very useful reaction, as long as you keep it under control!

A combustion reaction out of control

Burning fossil fuels

Some people still burn wood to heat their homes. But most people in Britain today use the **fossil fuels** coal, oil and gas. Even if your home is heated by electricity, fossil fuels were probably used in the power station to generate the electricity.

Coal is mostly the element carbon. When it burns, it produces the gas carbon dioxide.

$$\text{coal} + \text{oxygen} \xrightarrow{\text{combustion}} \text{carbon dioxide} + \text{energy}$$

Oil and gas contain compounds of carbon and hydrogen called **hydrocarbons**. When they burn in oxygen, the carbon turns to carbon dioxide and the hydrogen turns to water.

$$\text{oil or gas} + \text{oxygen} \longrightarrow \text{carbon dioxide} + \text{water} + \text{energy}$$

Fossil fuels formed from the remains of dead plants and animals. The plants made food and stored it, using energy from the Sun. When you burn a fossil fuel, the energy you get is from 'fossil sunshine'!

Coal is the remains of plants that grew millions of years ago.

Gas is another form of fossil sunshine.

Using fossil fuels

Fuels need a 'kick-start' of energy to get the reaction going. You need to light the fuel to start it burning. Some fuels are easier to light than others.

Coal is very hard to light, but it burns well, giving off lots of heat. You can store coal very safely.

Calor gas is very easy to light. You buy it in strong steel canisters that connect to cookers or heaters.

Wood is fairly easy to light, but you need a lot of wood to get a good fire. You can store dry wood safely.

Natural gas is very easy to light. People in towns and villages have the gas piped in to their homes.

a Which fuel would you use in each of these cases? Give as many reasons for your answers as you can.

1 cooking a meal on a survival course in the forest

2 cooking a meal at a campsite by the sea

3 cooking a meal in a high-rise flat

4 heating a country cottage 15 km from a town

5 running the central heating in a house in the town

6 for an open fire on cosy winter evenings in the town

What do you know?

1 Copy and complete the following sentences. Use the words below to fill the gaps.

| oxygen | energy | combustion | burn |

Fuels contain stored _____. This energy is released when they _____ in air. They react with the _____ in the air. This is called _____.

2 Write a word equation for:

a coal burning in air   **b** oil burning in air.

Key ideas

Fuels contain stored energy.

Fuels give out this energy when they burn in air. This reaction is called **combustion**.

The fossil fuels are coal, oil and gas.

Fuels need a 'kick-start' of energy to start the combustion reaction.

119

Chemicals in action

9d Acid rain

People are concerned about burning fossil fuels. What's the problem? Burning fuels produces carbon dioxide and water. These are the same chemicals that you breathe out.

Some people think that too much carbon dioxide in the air can make the Earth start to warm up (see page 133). Another problem is that fossil fuels are not pure.

When you speak, you put carbon dioxide and water into the atmosphere. Is this pollution?

Polluting the air

There are small amounts of sulphur in fossil fuels. When fuels burn, the sulphur reacts with oxygen to form sulphur dioxide gas:

sulphur + oxygen ⟶ sulphur dioxide

In the air, sulphur dioxide reacts with oxygen and rainwater. A weak solution of sulphuric acid is formed:

sulphur dioxide + oxygen + water ⟶ sulphuric acid

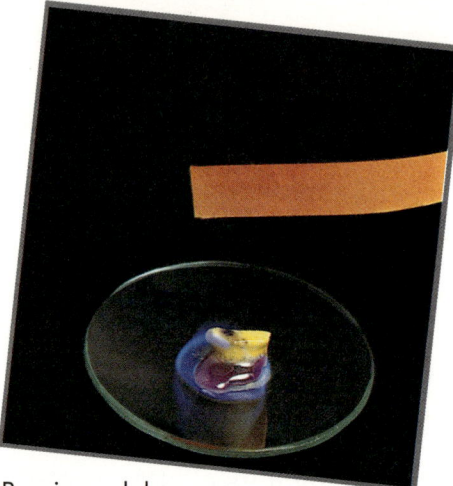

Burning sulphur produces an acidic gas.

Acid rain

Rain polluted with sulphur dioxide like this is called **acid rain**. Acid rain damages rocks and buildings. Pine trees are killed by acid rain because it affects the soil. Fish also die if lakes become too acidic.

Millions of tonnes of sulphur dioxide used to go into the air from power stations burning fossil fuels. The area near the power station was badly affected by acid rain, so they built tall chimneys. The gas was carried away by the wind. Unfortunately, this just meant that the acid rain fell somewhere else. Much of Britain's acid rain was blown to Norway!

The fish in many of Norway's rivers have been killed by acid rain from other countries.

What can we do?

Use less energy at home by turning off lights or turning the heating down a bit.

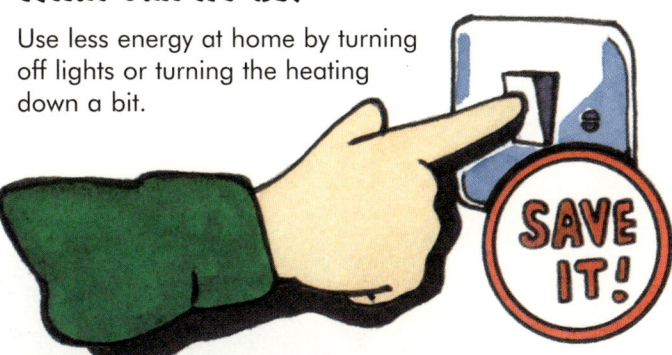

Walk, cycle or use public transport. Cars burn fossil fuels and cause lots of pollution.

What can scientists do?

Power stations have to clean up their waste gases by law. The gases are sprayed with water, which dissolves out the sulphur dioxide.

The fish in some Scottish lochs were killed by acid rain. Scientists neutralised the acidic water by adding lime. New fish have been put into the lochs.

What do you know?

1a How does acid rain form?
b Write a word equation for this reaction.
c What problems do acid rain cause?
d How can affected lakes be treated?

2 How do power stations treat their waste gases to help stop acid rain?

3 Design a poster to make people think about what they can do to reduce pollution. Point out any changes they could make to their own lifestyle.

Key ideas

Burning fossil fuels causes **acid rain**.

We can all help to reduce pollution by changing the way we live.

There are now laws which help to reduce pollution.

Scientists can reduce the problems caused by pollution.

Chemicals in action

9e Protecting metals

Sparklers are made from powdered iron glued onto wire. When you light a sparkler, the iron 'burns', giving off energy as heat and light. What is happening?

Metals and oxygen

The iron in the sparkler reacts with the oxygen in the air. It forms a compound called iron oxide. This reaction is called **oxidation**. The iron has been **oxidised** to form iron oxide. Most metals react with oxygen like this.

$$\text{metal} + \text{oxygen} \xrightarrow{\text{oxidation}} \text{metal oxide}$$

A useful oxidation

Aluminium is oxidised as soon as it meets the air. The aluminium oxide forms a thin but tough layer on the metal. This stops any more of the metal reacting. This is a useful oxidation, because the oxide layer protects the aluminium.

$$\text{aluminium} + \text{oxygen} \xrightarrow{\text{oxidation}} \text{aluminium oxide}$$

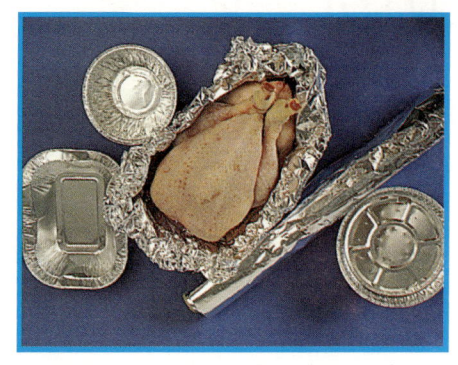

Aluminium has a surface layer of aluminium oxide.

A not-so-useful oxidation

The iron in a sparkler oxidises as it burns. But iron can also oxidise slowly without burning if there is water around. Iron reacts with oxygen and water to form **rust**.

$$\text{iron} + \text{oxygen} + \text{water} \xrightarrow{\text{oxidation}} \text{rust (iron oxide)}$$

Unfortunately, rust does not form a protective layer over the iron. Instead it swells and blisters off. This exposes fresh iron, which can react and form more rust . . . and so on.

Steel is made from iron with a little carbon. A solid piece of iron or steel can crumble into rust in just a few years.

Rusting is quicker if the weather is warm and damp.

Protecting against rust

Rust damage can be very expensive. If you can stop the air and water getting to the iron or steel, it cannot rust.

Cars are protected by many layers of tough paint. The paint is waterproof and airproof. But if the paint gets scratched or chipped, then rusting will start.

a Second-hand cars from Britain are often more badly rusted than those from desert countries like Libya. Why is this?

Tin cans?

'Tin cans' are made from steel coated with a thin layer of tin. Tin does not react with air and water. It prevents the air and water reaching the steel. Tin is not used on its own to make cans, because it is too soft and too expensive.

Stainless steel

You can prevent steel rusting by mixing chromium metal into it. It no longer reacts with air and water to form rust. Steel with chromium in it is called **stainless steel**. It is used to make cutlery.

Some cars are built from stainless steel, but they are very expensive.

b
1 Why aren't all cars made from stainless steel?

2 Car manufacturers might not want their cars to last twice as long. Why?

What do you know?

1 Copy and complete the following sentences. Use the words below to fill the gaps.

completely	blisters	oxygen
rust	iron	water

Iron reacts with _____ and _____ to form _____. Rust swells and _____, exposing fresh _____. In this way, iron objects can rust away _____ in time.

2 How does oxidation protect aluminium?

3 Why is it not a good idea to simply paint over rust spots on a car?

4a What are tin cans made from?
 b Why are they not made completely from tin?

Key ideas

Metals react with oxygen to form metal oxides. This is an **oxidation** reaction.

Aluminium oxide forms a tough layer on the surface of aluminium. This protects the aluminium from further attack.

Iron reacts with air and water to form **rust**. This blisters off so more iron underneath is exposed, and will rust.

Iron can be protected by layers of paint or tin.

Chemicals in action

9f Getting out the metals

Most metals are not found as elements. They are locked up in compounds in the rocks. These metal compounds are called **ores**. We need to get the metal out of its ore before we can use it.

Cassiterite is an ore of tin.

Pushing the other way

Many metal ores are oxides. When metals react with oxygen, energy is given out.

If you push enough energy back in, you can split the oxide up into the metal and oxygen. You could push energy in by heating the oxide to a very high temperature. Breaking up chemical compounds using heat like this is called **thermal decomposition**.

$$\text{metal oxide ore} + \text{heat energy} \xrightarrow{\text{thermal decomposition}} \text{metal} + \text{oxygen}$$

Getting mercury out by heating

Thermal decomposition works for mercury oxide.

$$\underset{\text{(red solid)}}{\text{mercury oxide}} + \text{heat energy} \longrightarrow \underset{\text{(silver liquid)}}{\text{mercury}} + \underset{\text{(colourless gas)}}{\text{oxygen}}$$

In mercury oxide, the metal and oxygen atoms are not held together too tightly. This is why you can split mercury oxide into mercury and oxygen just by heating it. But in other metal oxides, the metal and oxygen atoms are held together much more tightly. It is difficult to get them hot enough to get the metal out.

1 Red mercury oxide

2 Breaking up

3 Liquid mercury

Getting aluminium out by heating?

Aluminium is a very common metal. Mud is full of it! Aluminium oxide ore is called **bauxite**.

Aluminium atoms are held very tightly in aluminium oxide. You have to put lots of energy in to split the aluminium oxide. You would have to heat it to enormous temperatures. But energy costs money. The aluminium would be far more expensive than gold.

Getting aluminium out with electricity

Instead, the aluminium oxide is just heated until it melts. Then it is split by powerful electric currents. This gives aluminium metal.

The process is called **electrolysis**. It still takes quite a lot of energy. This is why aluminium is more expensive than iron, although it is more common.

Because aluminium is so difficult to get from its ores, it wasn't discovered until 1827. Napoleon was so impressed by this new 'wonder metal' that his best dinner service was made of aluminium rather than gold!

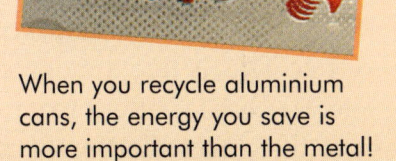

When you recycle aluminium cans, the energy you save is more important than the metal!

What do you know?

1 Copy and complete the following sentences. Use the words below to fill the gaps.

| ores | elements | oxygen |

Most metals are never found as _____ on Earth. They are usually locked up in compounds with other elements such as _____. These compounds are the metal _____.

2a What happens to red mercury oxide when it is heated?
b What is this type of reaction called?
c Why can't you get most metals from their compounds by heating?

3a How is aluminium split out from its oxide?
b Aluminium ore is quite cheap. Why is aluminium so expensive?
c Why is it important to recycle aluminium?

4 Why was aluminium only discovered fairly recently?

Key ideas

Most metals are found locked up in compounds called **ores**.

Compounds can be broken up by heating. This is called **thermal decomposition**.

You would need extremely high temperatures to get most metals from their compounds.

Aluminium is removed from its oxide using electrical energy instead of heat energy.

Chemicals in action

9g Pushing out the metals

You can get some metals from their ores by a process that's much cheaper than electrolysis.

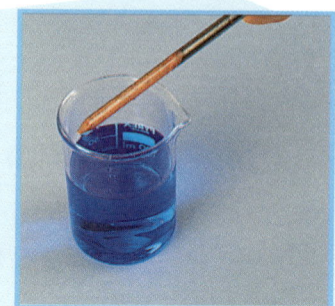

Chemical bullies

If you dip a clean iron nail into copper sulphate solution, it comes out coated with copper! The iron has pushed the copper out of its compound and taken its place. The iron is a 'chemical bully'.

iron + copper sulphate —displacement→ copper + iron sulphate

This reaction is called a **displacement** reaction. The iron displaces the copper. This is like a metal displacing hydrogen from an acid on page 91. Displacement reactions are used to push many metals out from their ores. Carbon is used as the 'chemical bully'.

Getting lead from its ore

Some metal ores are compounds with sulphur, called sulphides. The ore of lead is called **galena**. This is lead sulphide.

1 Galena is mined and crushed. It is roasted in air to turn it into lead oxide.

lead sulphide + oxygen —heat→ lead oxide + sulphur dioxide

2 Coal is roasted in closed ovens. It turns to **coke**. Coke is nearly pure carbon.

3 The lead oxide and coke are heated together in a furnace.

lead oxide + carbon —heat / displacement→ lead + carbon dioxide

4 The molten lead is run off.

Coal

Galena

Coke

Lead oxide

Lead

126

Getting iron from its ore

Iron oxide ore is usually used to make iron. Like lead, iron can be pushed out of its oxide by carbon. But iron needs much higher temperatures than lead. Iron is produced in a **blast furnace**.

Iron ore and coke are tipped in at the top.

In the middle, the carbon pushes the iron out of its oxide:

iron oxide + carbon $\xrightarrow{\text{displacement}}$ iron + carbon dioxide

At the bottom, coke burns in a blast of hot air. It heats the furnace to 1500 °C.

carbon + oxygen $\xrightarrow{\text{combustion}}$ carbon dioxide + heat energy

The molten iron runs out of the bottom.

Displacement uses much less energy than electrolysis. So iron is much cheaper than aluminium.

a The coke used in a blast furnace has two jobs. What are they?

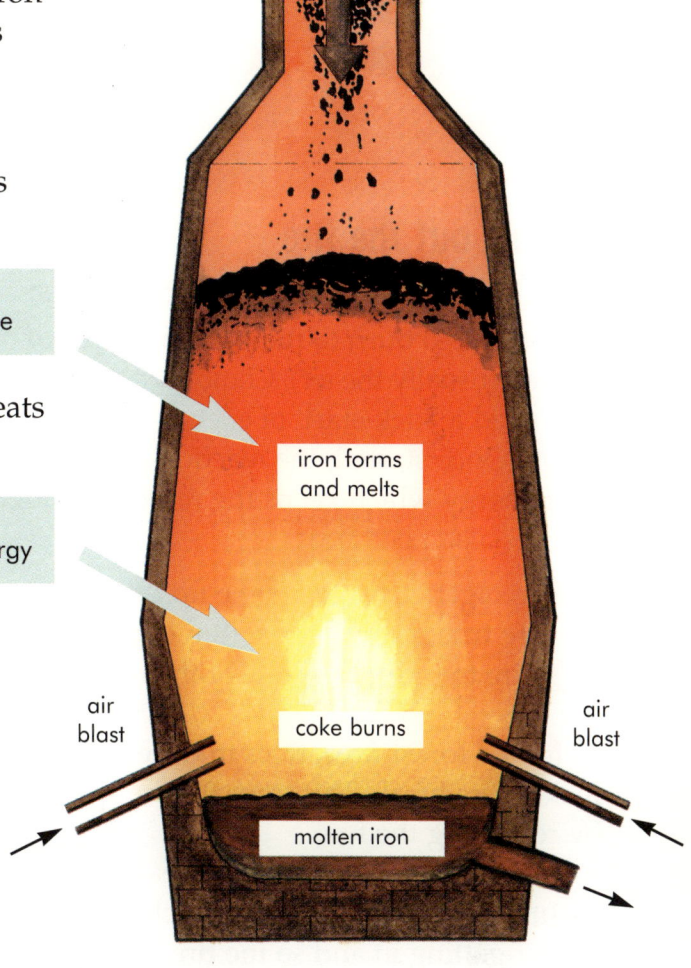

What do you know?

1a What happens when an iron nail is dipped into copper sulphate solution?
b What is this type of reaction called?
c Which element is used to push metals from their ores?

2 Write word equations for:
a roasting lead sulphide in air
b producing lead from lead oxide.

3 Coke reacts with oxygen from the air when it burns. Why do you think blasting air into the furnace makes it hotter?

4a Why is iron cheaper than aluminium?
b Aluminium is made by electrolysis. Do you think carbon could push aluminium from its ore?

Key ideas

One element can sometimes push another from its compounds. This is called **displacement**.

Carbon is used to push lead and iron from their oxides.

Displacement by carbon is the cheapest way to get metals from their oxides.

Chemicals in action

9 EXTRAS

9c Putting out the fire

Fires are combustion reactions. They need something to burn (a fuel) and a source of oxygen (usually the air). Combustion reactions also need a 'kick-start' of energy to get them going. Once started, the reaction produces heat energy which keeps the reaction going. So fires also need heat.

Fuel, oxygen and heat make up the sides of the **fire triangle**. All three things are needed for a fire to burn. Take one of them away and the fire will go out.
- In bad forest fires, trees may be felled to make a fire-break. This stops the fire spreading by removing the fuel.
- Wrapping a fire blanket or heavy coat around someone with burning clothes stops the air getting in and so the fire goes out.
- Some fires can be put out using water. As the water boils away, it cools the fire down. The fire goes out.

1 Use the fire triangle to explain how the following firefighting ideas work:
a A damp cloth or blanket should be put over a burning chip pan.
b Red fire extinguishers are used to squirt water onto burning litter bins.
c Aircraft are covered with carbon dioxide foam if they crash-land.
d A small fire can be put out by covering the burning material with sand.

9d The new London smog

In the 1950s, London was plagued by thick black smog which killed thousands of people. It was caused by soot and waste gases from coal fires that got caught up in fog. To stop this, people were banned from using coal fires in London. London has been free of this type of smog ever since.

A 'pea-souper' smog from the 1950s

128

Now London is being smothered by a new kind of smog. Millions of cars pass through London every day. Their exhaust pipes pump soot, carbon monoxide, hydrocarbons and nitrogen oxides into the air.

All these gases then react with the air itself. The reactions are triggered by sunlight. The result is a brown haze in the air that is called **photochemical smog**. It can make your eyes sting and badly affects people with breathing problems. It also seems to make asthma far worse.

This smog may not be so easy to cure. In Athens, where the problem is even worse, cars are not allowed to enter the city on bad days.

1a What caused the smog in the 1950s?
b How was this terrible pollution stopped?
2a What causes the smog today?
b Suggest some ways of reducing the smog problem in London.

9g Putting metals in order

Displacing a metal from its ore by carbon is relatively cheap, and works well for many metals. Getting aluminium from its ore by electrolysis is very expensive. Why is aluminium not displaced by carbon too? The answer is that the displacement reaction does not work with aluminium. Why not?

Carbon acts as a 'chemical bully', pushing metals such as copper or iron from their compounds. Carbon is more reactive than copper and iron. But aluminium is more reactive than carbon. So this displacement reaction cannot work, and expensive electrolysis is the only alternative.

more reactive	sodium	
	magnesium	metals produced by electrolysis
	aluminium	
	carbon	------------------------------------
	zinc	
	iron	metals produced by
	lead	carbon displacement
less reactive	copper	

1 Why is an iron nail able to push copper out of copper sulphate?
2 Tin is produced by carbon displacement. Is tin more or less reactive than carbon?
3 Potassium is produced by electrolysis. Is potassium more or less reactive than carbon?
4 What would happen if magnesium ribbon was put into lead nitrate solution?

Energy resources

10a Ancient energy

Trees need energy to grow. They get their energy from sunlight. As they grow, some of the energy from the sunlight is stored in the wood they make. This is the process of photosynthesis.

If you make a wood fire, you burn the wood. You get heat energy and light energy from the wood. This energy came from the sunlight that fell on the tree when it was growing. Wood from trees which were growing recently is called **biomass fuel**.

a A tree changes light energy into stored chemical energy. Draw an energy transfer diagram to show this.

Black rock

Coal is a useful fuel. In some places, it is near the surface of the Earth. People dig it out of a big pit. In other places, it is deep underground, and people mine it using giant machines.

Coal is formed from plants which lived hundreds of millions of years ago. When the plants died, they were gradually squashed by rocks which formed on top of them. The plants became fossils, so coal is known as a **fossil fuel**.

When we burn coal, the chemical energy from the dead plants is changed to heat energy and light energy, just as it is when we burn wood.

Oil and gas

As well as coal, we use two other fossil fuels, oil and gas. They formed from the remains of sea creatures which lived hundreds of millions of years ago. Sometimes oil and gas are found under land. Sometimes they are found under the sea. Most of the oil and gas used in the UK comes from under the North Sea.

Fossil fuels are useful for burning because they give us more energy than wood.

The picture shows how much energy in kJ (kilojoules) is stored in 1 g of each type of fuel.

▶ **b** Write the fuels in order, starting with the one which stores least energy.

wood 20 kJ   coal 27 kJ   gas 55 kJ
charcoal 34 kJ   oil 42 kJ

Fuels for the future

Eventually, all the fossil fuels in the Earth may be used up. Fossil fuels are **non-renewable**. We will need to find new sources of energy.

Some farmers are growing trees for firewood. Instead of growing food for us to eat, they are growing fuel for us to burn.

When the trees have been cut down, new ones can be grown. Wood is a **renewable** fuel.

What do you know?

1 Copy and complete the following table. Use the words below to fill the boxes.

wood	gas	sunlight	oil	coal

fossil fuels	
not a fossil fuel	
where trees get their energy from	

2 Copy and complete the following sentences. Use the word **renewable** or **non-renewable** to fill the gaps.

We cut down trees and burn the wood. We can always plant more trees, so wood is a _____ fuel. When we have burnt the last lump of coal, there will be never be any more. Coal is a _____ fuel.

3 Draw an energy transfer diagram to show how the light energy from a log fire originally came from the Sun.

Key ideas

Wood has been used as a fuel for a very long time. We also use **fossil fuels** (coal, oil and gas). These store energy which came from the Sun millions of years ago.

People are always looking for new supplies of fossil fuels. Eventually they will run out. Fossil fuels are **non-renewable**.

Energy resources

10b Island in the Sun

Have you ever wished that you lived on an island where the Sun is always shining? Well, you do! The 'island' is the Earth. The Earth is like an island in space, and the Sun is always shining on the Earth.

a Why don't we always see the Sun? (Give as many reasons as you can.)

Energy from the Sun

We get most of our energy from the Sun. We can see the light it gives us, and we can feel its heat on our skin.

You may have a calculator that works from sunlight. There is a solar cell in the calculator. The cell changes light energy from the Sun into electrical energy.

This strange car drove all the way across Australia using energy from the Sun. It has solar cells which change light energy into electrical energy. It has an electric motor which changes the electrical energy into movement energy.

b What is the scientific name for movement energy?

Under the blanket

The Sun's rays warm the Earth. The Earth is surrounded by its atmosphere, the air we breathe. The atmosphere helps to keep the Earth warm. It makes it difficult for heat to escape from the Earth. The atmosphere is like a giant blanket all round the Earth. The way it keeps the Earth warm is called the **greenhouse effect**.

The Moon is about 40 °C colder than the Earth. It doesn't have an atmosphere to keep it warm. There is no greenhouse effect on the Moon.

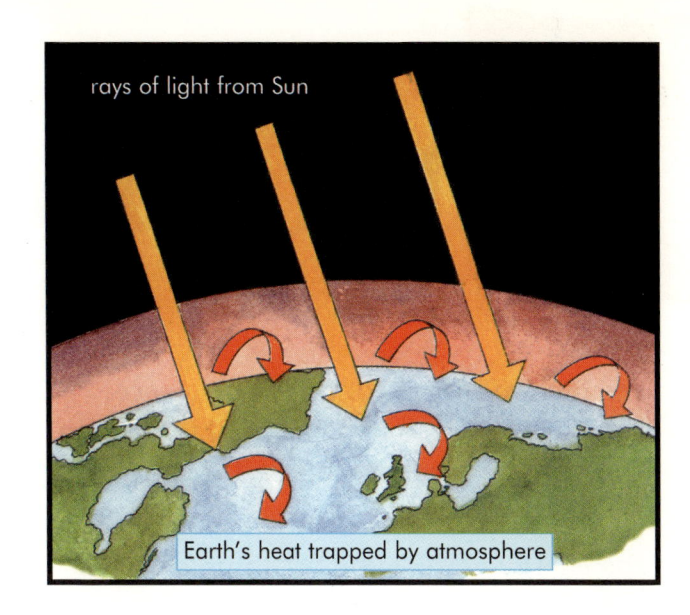

Getting warmer

This equation describes what happens when we burn a fuel:

$$\text{fuel} + \text{oxygen} \longrightarrow \text{new chemicals} + \text{energy}$$

c Is this a chemical change or a physical change? Give a reason for your answer.

One of the new chemicals made is carbon dioxide. This gas goes into the atmosphere. It makes the 'blanket' thicker. Many scientists think that this is making the Earth warmer.

If we burn all of the Earth's fossil fuels, the Earth may get too warm. Ice at the Poles may melt, so the level of the sea may rise and cause flooding. The weather may change, and new deserts may form.

What do you know?

1a Name two kinds of energy we get from the Sun.
b How can energy from the Sun be changed to electrical energy?

2 The Earth's atmosphere lets rays of light from the Sun reach the Earth's surface. The atmosphere makes it difficult for heat to escape. Why do you think this is called the greenhouse effect?

3 Draw an energy transfer diagram to show the energy changes for the solar car in the photograph on the opposite page.

Key ideas

Most of our energy comes from the Sun.

The atmosphere is like a blanket around the Earth, helping to keep it warm. This is called the **greenhouse effect**. If we burn all the Earth's fossil fuels, there will be much more carbon dioxide in the atmosphere. The Earth may get too warm.

Energy resources

10c Wet and windy

The picture shows windmills in Greece. The hillside seems to be covered with them. The farmers use them to grind corn and to crush olives.

The energy of the wind is captured by the sails of the windmill. The sails turn the machinery inside the mill.

a What kind of energy does the wind have?

Sun and wind

The energy of the wind comes from the Sun. The Sun's rays warm up the atmosphere. When air gets hot, it expands and becomes less dense. It floats upwards.

There are areas of cold air around. Cold air is more dense. It sinks to replace the hot air. This movement of air is what we call wind.

If you look back at the picture of the Earth seen from space (page 48), you can see the pattern of the swirling atmosphere.

The wind's energy can be used to generate electricity. A big wind generator can provide enough electrical energy for a village. The small generator in the photograph is used to run the lights and refrigerator in the canal boat.

b In what way is this generator similar to the windmills in the photograph at the top of the page? In what way is it different?

134

Wind and waves

When the wind blows across the sea, it makes waves.
When the wind stops blowing, the waves soon die down.

c What force causes the waves to appear as the wind blows across the surface of the sea?

The water cycle

- clouds form
- rain falls
- streams run downhill
- watermill
- water vapour rises and cools
- Sun's rays warm the sea

When water runs downhill, it has two kinds of energy, kinetic and gravitational.

We can make use of the energy of a river by making it turn a wheel. This might turn machinery for a mill, or it might generate electricity.

The Sun keeps shining, so water keeps moving around the water cycle. Energy from water is a renewable source of energy.

What do you know?

1 Copy and complete the following table. Use the types of energy below to fill the boxes.

| kinetic | heat | electrical |
| gravitational | light | |

energy of moving water	
energy of water high up	
energy from the Sun	
energy from a generator	

2 How might the weather affect someone who uses a wind turbine to generate their electricity?

Key ideas

Energy from the Sun drives the water cycle. It makes the wind blow. The wind makes waves.

We can get energy from all of these sources. Because the Sun keeps shining, they are always available. They are renewable energy sources.

Energy resources

10d The great escape

In the UK, we have to heat our homes to make them comfortable to live in. Because it is colder outside than inside, heat energy tends to escape.

a Make a list of all the different ways in which heat energy is escaping from this house.

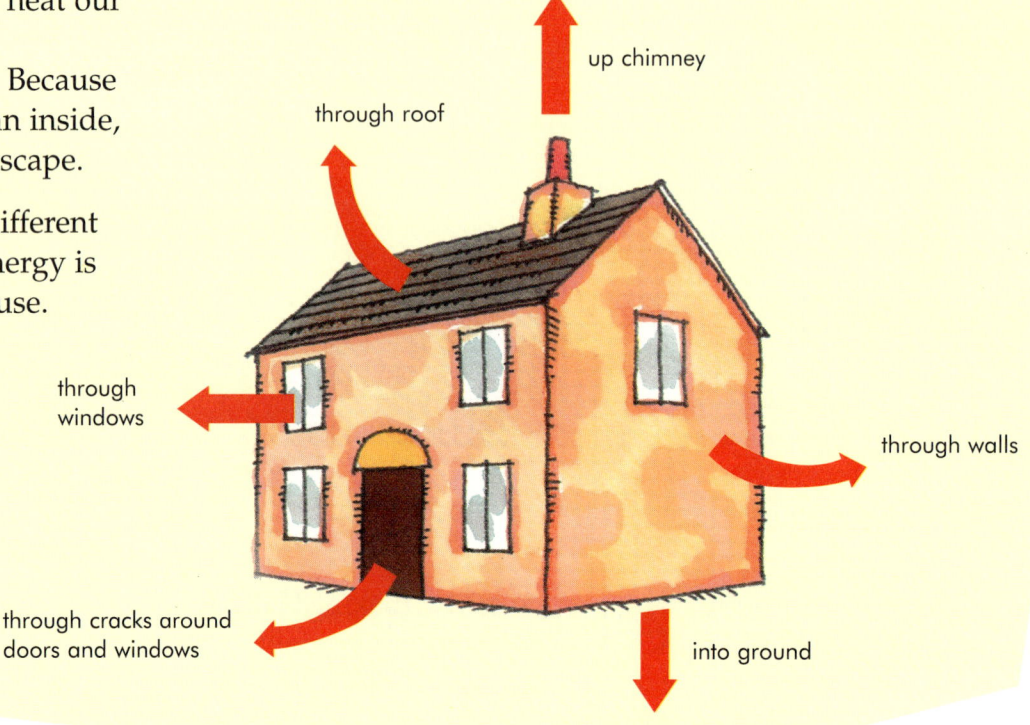

Labels on house diagram: up chimney, through roof, through windows, through walls, through cracks around doors and windows, into ground

Energy costs money

It isn't just heat energy that is being wasted when it escapes from your home. Energy costs money, so money is being wasted too.

b Look at the table. Which energy supply is the cheapest? Which is the most expensive?

We can make better use of our energy, and waste less money, by trying to stop heat escaping from our homes.

If we waste less energy, the Earth's reserves of fossil fuels will last longer. And our fuel bills will be smaller, too.

Energy supply	Energy supplied for 1p
coal	1500 kJ
gas	2400 kJ
oil	2600 kJ
electricity	500 kJ

Saving energy, saving money

On a cold night, we snuggle down under the bedclothes. Blankets or a duvet help to stop the heat of our bodies escaping.

A house needs a 'blanket' too, to keep it warm. Loft insulation stops heat escaping through the roof. Double glazing stops it escaping through the windows. Loft insulation and double glazing are two ways of saving energy.

The photographs show what you can see if you look closely at a blanket and loft insulation. They are both made of fibres. Air is trapped in between the fibres. Heat energy cannot escape easily through these materials. They are **insulating materials**.

c Some people have a thick duvet for the winter and a thin duvet for the summer. Why do they want a thinner duvet for the summer?

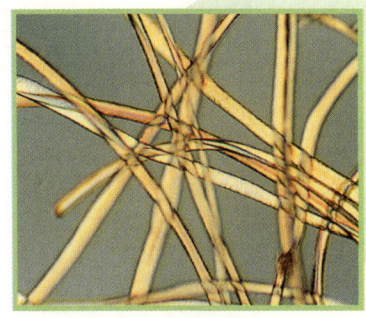

Loft insulation

Blanket

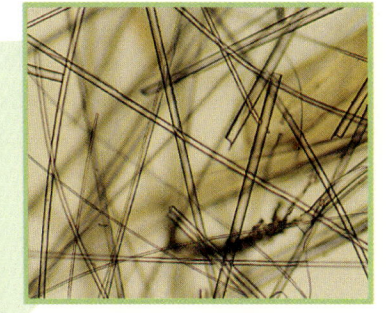

What do you know?

1 Copy and complete the following sentences. Use the words below to fill the gaps.

| energy | hot | escape | materials |

Heat energy tends to _____ from things that are _____. Insulating _____ help stop the heat _____ escaping.

2 Draw a bar chart to show the amount of energy you get for 1p from different energy supplies. Use the information in the table on the opposite page.

3 The Inuit people of northern Canada live in arctic conditions. They wear thick furs. It can be very warm inside their houses, which are built of thick ice. Write a paragraph to explain how the Inuits make good use of insulating materials.

Key ideas

It is difficult to keep things hot because heat energy is always escaping.

Heat energy that escapes is wasted.

Energy resources

10e Hotter and colder

The car engine is hot. It is much hotter than its surroundings. Heat energy escapes from it and warms up the surroundings.

Your skin is sensitive to heat energy. If you put your hands near a mug of hot drink, you can feel the heat energy escaping.

Honest, Guv. I've been in front of the telly all night.

I can feel heat escaping from the hot engine!

From hotter to colder

Heat energy escapes from anything that is hotter than its surroundings. The arrows show how the heat energy is moving from the hot drink to the air round about, which is colder than the drink. The heat energy does not disappear. It is just more spread out.

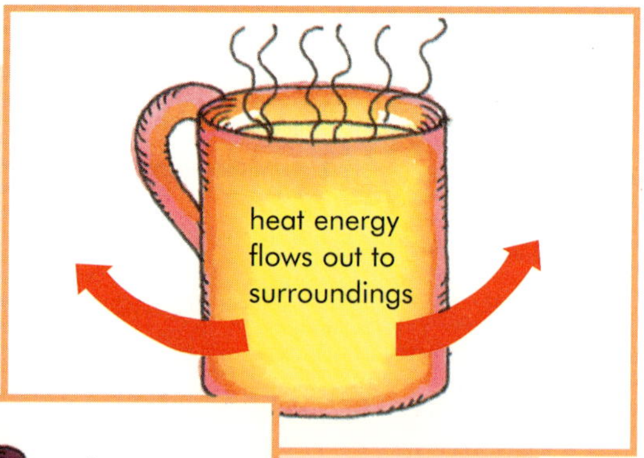

The snowman is made of cold snow. The Sun has started to shine, and the surroundings have warmed up. Now heat energy moves from the warm surroundings into the cold snowman.

heat energy flows out to surroundings

heat energy flows in from surroundings

a How can you tell that heat energy is moving into the snowman?

138

Body temperature

Human beings need to keep warm. The **temperature** of our bodies is usually about 37 °C. We use a thermometer to tell us how hot we are. It measures our temperature.

If you go outside on a cold day, heat energy will escape from your body. Soon you will start to feel cold.

Your body is warmer than its surroundings. Heat energy flows from your body (which is hotter) to the air (which is cooler).

You can get warm again by lying in a hot bath. Now your body is cooler than its surroundings. Heat energy flows into your body from the hot bath water.

▶ **b** How can we make it difficult for heat energy to escape from our bodies on a cold day?

What do you know?

1 Copy and complete the following sentences. Choose from the words below to fill the gaps.

| colder | hotter | energy |
| hot | | temperature |

The _____ of something tells us how _____ it is. Heat _____ tends to escape from something which is _____ than its surroundings.

2 Look around the room. Make a list of all the things in the room that are warmer than their surroundings. Is there anything that is colder than its surroundings?

3 What happens if you leave a cold drink on the table on a warm day? Draw a diagram to show how heat energy flows.

4 An ornithologist was investigating the temperature of an egg in a bird's nest. The bird flew away to feed, and then came back. The graph shows what the ornithologist found out.

a What was the temperature of the egg when the bird was sitting on it?
b What happened when the bird flew away?
c What happened when the bird came back?

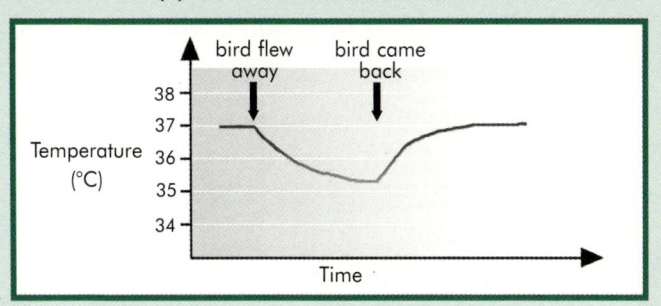

Key ideas

The **temperature** of something tells us how hot it is.

When something is hotter than its surroundings, heat energy escapes from it. As it loses energy, its temperature becomes lower.

The escaping heat energy spreads out and warms up the surroundings.

Energy resources 10

EXTRAS

10a Energy explanations

In each of the sentences below, some of the words are in bold. Write a paragraph for each sentence to explain the meanings of the bold words.

1 Wood is a **renewable** source of energy.

2 Gas is a **concentrated** store of energy. Wood is not such a concentrated store.

3 The energy from burning coal is **ancient** energy. The energy from burning wood is **recent** energy.

10b Energy equations

Here are two scientific equations:

> A carbon dioxide + water + energy ⟶ sugar + oxygen
>
> B fuel + oxygen ⟶ carbon dioxide + water + energy

1 Which equation represents what happens when something burns?

2 Which equation represents photosynthesis?

3 Where does photosynthesis happen?

4 Some people say that burning is the 'opposite' of photosynthesis. What do you think they mean by this?

10c Beach breezes

If you go to the beach, you may notice that there is often a breeze blowing. Sometimes it blows from the land to the sea, and sometimes from the sea to the land.

1 This diagram shows how the breeze blows in the evening. The Sun has been shining, and the land is much warmer than the sea. Use the diagram to help you explain why the breeze blows from the sea to the land in the evening.

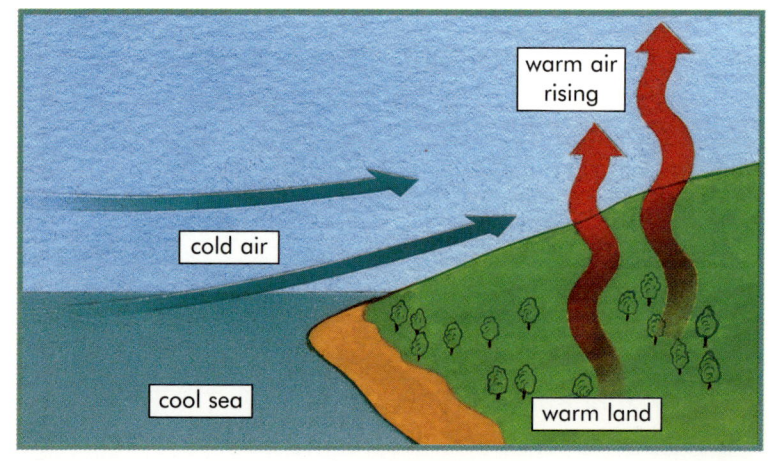

2 At night, the land cools down much faster than the sea. In the morning, a breeze blows from the land to the sea. Copy and complete the diagram. Use it to help you explain why the breeze blows this way in the morning.

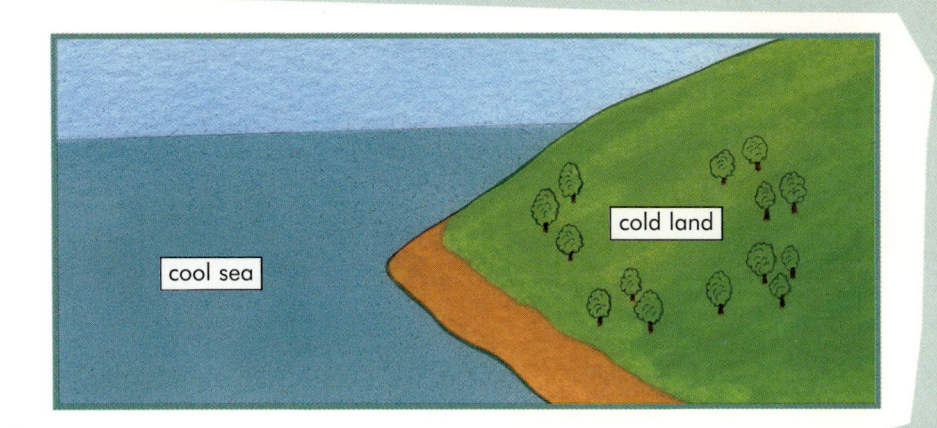

10d Waste not

The picture shows a house that is heated by gas central heating. You can see what happens to every 1000 J of energy that started off stored in the gas.

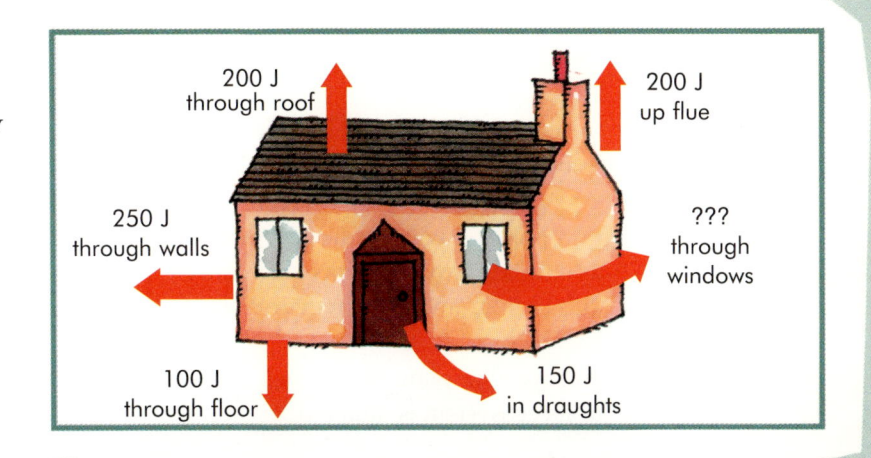

1 How much heat energy escapes through the glass of the windows?
2 Draw an energy transfer diagram to show what happens to each 1000 J of energy from the gas.

10e Cooling off

Some pupils were investigating how heat energy escapes from a beaker of hot water. They had three beakers. They filled each with 100 cm^3 of boiling water from a kettle. They put a temperature probe in each.

beaker 1	no insulation, no lid
beaker 2	insulation, no lid
beaker 3	insulation, lid

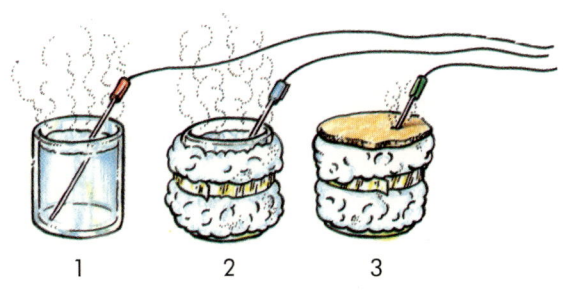

The computer screen shows a graph of how the temperature of each beaker changed.

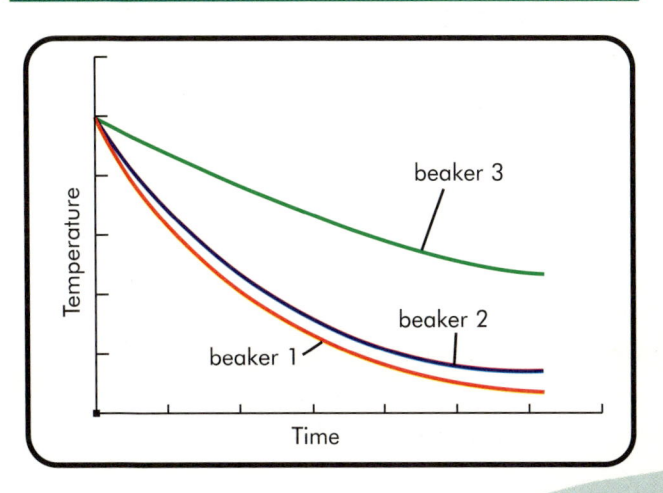

1 What conclusions would you draw from this experiment?

Glossary

absorbed
page 100

digested food molecules are absorbed when they pass from the small intestine to the blood.

acid
pages 78–93, 98

a chemical that has a sour taste. Acids react with bases, and strong acids are corrosive. Acids have a pH less than 7.

acid indigestion
page 82

burning feeling caused by acid bubbling up out of your stomach.

acid rain
pages 120–1

rain polluted with acidic gases such as sulphur dioxide, which eats away at buildings and kills trees and fish.

adapted
pages 50–3

an animal or plant that is well suited to its ecosystem is adapted.

alkali
pages 79–83, 92–3

a chemical that dissolves in water and reacts with an acid. Alkalis have a pH greater than 7.

alveoli
pages 10, 11, 12, 13

tiny air sacs that make up the lungs.

amino acids
page 98

small molecules formed when proteins are digested.

amylase
page 105

an enzyme in saliva that breaks down starch.

antacid
page 82

medicine for acid indigestion, that neutralises excess stomach acid.

antagonistic muscles
page 4

a pair of muscles that work against each other to move a bone.

anus
page 101

ring of muscle at the end of the gut. Faeces are passed out of the body through the anus.

arteries
pages 16, 17, 20

blood vessels that carry blood from your heart all over your body.

atom
pages 22–3, 24, 34

the smallest particle of an element. Molecules are made up of atoms joined together.

attracting
pages 36–7, 38

pulling together, e.g. two magnets with opposite poles together will attract each other.

axis
page 71

a line passing through the Earth from the North Pole to the South Pole. The Earth spins on its axis.

balanced forces
pages 111, 113

forces are balanced when they cancel each other out. The object remains stationary or continues to move at a steady speed.

base
pages 82, 84–5

a chemical that reacts with an acid. Soluble bases are called alkalis.

bauxite
page 125

aluminium oxide ore.

biomass
pages 55, 64

the amount of biological material in an organism.

biomass fuel
page 130

fuel from plants that were growing recently. Wood is a biomass fuel.

blast furnace
page 127

a large furnace used to extract iron from its ore.

blood vessels
pages 16, 17
tubes that carry blood around your body.

bronchi
page 8
two branches of the windpipe that lead to the lungs.

capillaries
page 17
tiny blood vessels connecting your arteries to your veins.

carbohydrates
pages 94, 105
food substances that we need for energy.

carnivore
pages 60, 62, 104
an animal that eats other animals.

cartilage
page 5
tough rubbery tissue that covers the ends of bones.

cellulase
page 104
an enzyme needed in order to digest cellulose from plants.

chemical reaction
pages 26–7, 98, 114–29
a change that forms a new substance, and cannot easily change back.

chemical weathering
page 89
the breaking down of rocks by chemical reactions with rainwater and air.

cilia
pages 8, 13
small hair-like parts of cells. In the respiratory system, cilia move dirt up away from the lungs.

coke
pages 126, 127
a form of carbon used to extract some metals from their ores. Coke is formed by roasting coal in an oven to purify it.

collecting over water
page 90
collecting a gas by bubbling it through water into a collecting tube.

combustion
pages 118–19, 128
a chemical reaction in which a substance burns. It reacts with oxygen, producing a flame and giving out heat energy.

compass
pages 40, 44, 66
this has a magnetic needle that swings so one end of it points north.

competition
pages 60–1
organisms compete with each other for what they need, e.g. animals compete for food and mates, plants compete for light.

compound
pages 27, 28–9
a substance made of two or more different kinds of atoms chemically joined together.

consumer
page 54
an animal which eats (consumes) plants or other animals.

contracting
page 4
a muscle getting shorter, so it can pull on a bone.

corrosive
page 78
a chemical that eats away at many materials it touches.

digestion
pages 95–101, 104–5
breaking food substances down into small molecules that can pass into your blood.

digestive system
pages 95–7, 104
the long tube that breaks down your food and takes it into your blood, and the organs that go with it.

displacing
pages 91, 126–7, 129
pushing a substance out from its compound, e.g. a metal displaces hydrogen from an acid. The metal takes the place of the hydrogen in the acid.

dormant
page 52
an animal or plant that slows down its life processes, e.g. for the winter, has become dormant.

ecosystem
page 49
all the different things that affect an animal or plant's home. The other animals and plants, the weather and the type of soil all make up the ecosystem.

egestion
page 101
passing waste out of the body.

electrolysis
pages 125, 129
a process used to get aluminium from its ore. An electric current is passed through the molten ore.

electromagnet pages 42–5, 47	a magnet that works by electricity. An electric current flows through a coil of wire. You can switch it on and off.
element pages 24–5, 32–3	a substance made of only one kind of atom.
environment page 58	the physical surroundings an organism lives with, e.g. temperature or amount of water.
enzyme pages 98–9	a substance formed in the body that speeds up a chemical reaction, e.g. in digestion.
faeces pages 101, 104	semi-solid waste left at the end of digestion.
fats page 94	food substances that we need to supply and store energy.
fire triangle page 128	fuel, oxygen and heat make up the sides of the fire triangle. Removing one side of the triangle puts out the fire.
fossil fuel pages 118–19, 130–1	fuel that formed over millions of years from the remains of living things. Coal, oil and gas are fossil fuels.
fuel pages 118–19, 130–1	a substance that gives out a lot of heat energy when it is burned, e.g. coal, oil, gas, wood.
galena page 126	lead sulphide ore.
gas exchange page 10	passing oxygen from the air to the blood, and carbon dioxide from the blood to the air.
greenhouse effect page 133	the way the atmosphere keeps the Earth warm, like a giant blanket.
habitat pages 48–9	the place where an animal or plant lives.
hard water page 88	water that contains a dissolved calcium salt.
herbivore pages 60, 62, 104	an animal that eats only plants.
hibernating page 52	remaining inactive through the winter.
high blood pressure pages 20, 21	a higher pressure than normal inside your blood vessels.
hydrocarbons page 118	compounds containing only carbon and hydrogen, found in oil or gas.
indicator pages 80–1	a chemical that is one colour in an alkali and a different colour in an acid.
insulating materials page 137	materials that prevent heat escaping, e.g. loft insulation.
joint pages 3, 5	a place where bones meet and move over each other.
ligament page 5	strong strap that holds the bones together in a joint.
light gate page 109	apparatus used to measure speed.
lines of force page 39	lines that we draw around a magnet to show the magnetic field pattern.
litmus page 80	an indicator that is red in acids and blue in alkalis.
lubricating page 5	stopping moving parts rubbing on each other, e.g. oil lubricates a car engine.
magnetic field pages 38–9, 40–1, 43, 46	an area around a magnet. Magnetic materials will be attracted or repelled if you put them in this area.
magnetic materials page 37	substances that are attracted by a magnet, e.g. iron and steel.

managing pages 56–7, 65	we manage a food chain when we control or change it, e.g. growing animals or plants for food.	**oxidised** page 122	a chemical has been oxidised when it has reacted with oxygen to form an oxide.
microhabitat page 64	a little habitat, e.g. a rock pool.	**peristalsis** page 96	the muscles of the gut squeeze the food along by contracting in waves.
mitochondria page 102	small structures in cells, in which respiration takes place.	**pesticide** pages 56–7	a chemical that kills insect pests.
mixture pages 26, 30–1	different types of atoms or molecules which are not joined together chemically and so can easily be separated.	**pH scale** page 81	scale of numbers from 1 (strongest acid) through 7 (neutral) to 14 (strongest alkali).
molecule pages 22–3, 27, 34, 99	a particle made up of more than one atom joined together.	**photochemical smog** page 129	gases in the air that react in sunlight to form a brown haze of pollution.
neutral page 81	a substance that is neither acidic nor alkaline is neutral, e.g. pure water. Neutral substances have a pH of 7.	**physical process** pages 26, 98, 116	a change that can easily change back, e.g. dissolving or evaporating.
neutralisation pages 82, 83, 84, 86–7, 92	a chemical reaction between an acid and a base that produces a neutral solution.	**plasma** page 15	a pale yellow liquid that carries chemicals and helps to form clots when you cut yourself. Plasma makes up a large part of the blood.
non-renewable page 131	energy sources that are used up are non-renewable, e.g. fossil fuels.	**platelets** page 15	tiny bits of cells in the blood that help to form clots when you cut yourself.
north-seeking pole page 40	the end of a magnet that swings to point north.	**polymer** page 34	a chemical such as polythene, with big molecules formed by joining lots of little molecules together.
orbit pages 68, 69, 70, 77	the path of a planet as it travels round the Sun.	**population** pages 58–9	a group of organisms of the same species living in the same habitat.
ore pages 124–7, 129	a compound of a metal found in rocks. A metal can be extracted from its ore.	**population density** page 65	when lots of organisms in a population live very close together, the population density is high.
organic compounds page 29	lots of different compounds containing carbon and hydrogen with other elements such as oxygen and nitrogen. Organic compounds make up all living things.	**predator** page 53	an animal that hunts and eats other animals (its prey).
		prey page 53	an animal that is hunted by a predator for food.
oxidation page 122	a chemical reaction in which a substance reacts with oxygen to form an oxide.	**producer** page 54	a plant which produces its own food by photosynthesis.

products page 117	the new substances formed in a chemical reaction.	**rust** pages 122–3	an oxide of iron formed with air and water. Rusting causes iron and steel to corrode.
proteins page 94	food substances that we need for growing and repairing damaged cells.	**saliva** page 96	a liquid produced in the mouth that makes food easier to swallow, and starts off digestion.
pure pages 30–1, 35	a substance that contains only one compound or element is pure. All its particles are the same.	**salt** pages 84–5	a chemical formed when an acid reacts with a base.
pyramid of numbers pages 54–5	a diagram that shows how many organisms there are at each level of a food chain.	**satellite** page 74	something that travels round a planet, e.g. the Moon or a spacecraft.
raw materials pages 114–15	natural materials, e.g. rock or wood, that we change to make products.	**silica** page 32	a compound of silicon and oxygen. Sand is a form of silica.
reactants page 117	the substances that react together in a chemical reaction.	**sodium chloride** pages 28, 85	the chemical name for common salt.
red blood cells page 15	cells in the blood that carry oxygen.	**soil** pages 83, 89	a mixture of different particles formed by the breakdown of rocks.
relaxing page 4	a muscle no longer contracting, so it can be pulled back to its original shape.	**solar system** pages 68–9	the Sun and the group of planets that travel round the Sun.
relay page 45	a switch that works using an electromagnet.	**species** page 48	type of animal or plant. Animals or plants from one species can breed together, but not with other species.
renewable pages 131, 134–5	energy sources that can be replaced are renewable, e.g. wood, solar power, wind power.	**speed** pages 106-13	how fast something is moving. Speed=distance moved/time taken.
repelling pages 36–7, 38	pushing apart, e.g. two magnets with like poles together will repel each other.	**stainless steel** page 123	a metal made of steel with chromium, that does not rust.
respiration pages 102–3	a chemical reaction that happens in your cells to release energy. The reaction uses oxygen and glucose, and produces water, carbon dioxide and usable energy.	**stalactite** page 88	a limestone needle hanging down from the roof of a cave.
		stalagmite page 88	a limestone column growing up from the floor of a cave.
respiratory system pages 8–13	your lungs and the tubes connecting them to your nose and mouth. Your respiratory system is used for gas exchange.	**strong acid** pages 78, 81	an acid that is very corrosive, e.g. hydrochloric acid.
		symbol page 33	a shorthand for the elements. Each element has a symbol of one or two letters.

synovial fluid
page **5**

a liquid that cushions and lubricates the bones inside joints which move a lot.

temperature
pages **52, 58, 72, 139, 141**

how hot something is, measured with a thermometer.

tendon
page **4**

this attaches the end of a muscle to a bone.

thermal decomposition
page **124**

breaking down a compound by heating it.

tissue
page **4**

a group of similar cells all working together, e.g. muscle or bone

unbalanced forces
pages **111, 113**

forces are unbalanced when one is bigger than another. This causes the object to speed up or slow down.

uncombined
pages **32, 35**

a substance that is found in the Earth as an element, instead of in a compound, is uncombined.

universal indicator
page **81**

an indicator that has a range of colours showing the strength of an acid or alkali on the pH scale.

veins
pages **16, 17**

blood vessels that carry blood from all over your body back to your heart.

villi
page **100**

finger-like structures in the small intestine that help digested food molecules pass into your blood.

weak acid
pages **78, 81**

an acid that is not very corrosive, e.g. citric acid.

white blood cells
page **15**

cells in the blood that defend against disease.

windpipe
page **8**

tube leading from the mouth and nose down to the lungs.